THE WAR OF
INDEPENDENCE
IN KILDARE

THE WAR OF INDEPENDENCE IN KILDARE

James Durney

MERCIER PRESS
IRISH PUBLISHER – IRISH STORY

MERCIER PRESS

Cork

www.mercierpress.ie

© James Durney, 2013

ISBN: 978 1 78117 166 0

10 9 8 7 6 5 4 3 2 1

A CIP record for this title is available from the British Library

Printed and bound in the EU.

CONTENTS

'We solemnly declare foreign government in Ireland to be an invasion of our national right …'

Declaration of Independence, Dáil Éireann, 21 January 1919

Dedicated to:

William Gaul, Rathasker Road, Naas, County Kildare
(Naas Labour Union)

and

James Durney, OC E Company (IRA), Mullinavat,
County Kilkenny, War of Independence

Dublin
to Sligo

Kilcock

Maynooth

Leixlip

Carbury

Celbridge

Prosperous

Clane

Robertstown

Sallins

Kil

Kilteel

Rathangan

Greenhills

Naas

Newbridge

Dublin to
Limerick
and Cork

Curragh Camp

Ballymore-
Eustace

Kildare

Kilcullen

Monasterevin

Ballitore

Athy

Barrowhouse

Railway

Ambush

Castledermot

Dublin to
Waterford

Courtesy of J. Durney/M. Corrigan

ACKNOWLEDGEMENTS

This book would not have been written without the help and contributions of so many people over the years. My big thanks to the Local Studies, Genealogy and Archives Department, Newbridge, where much of the material was sourced. My thanks to a wonderful editorial team: Mary Feehan and Wendy Logue; as always, to Commandant Laing (retired) and the excellent staff at the Military Archives, Dublin; my son, Brian, for drawing the escape map from the Rath Camp; my friend and work colleague Mario Corrigan, a great editor who keeps driving me on; Karel Kiely, Genealogy Department, Newbridge, for her answers to my many queries; my late great-aunt Ellen Gaul, who filled my head with stories of Naas during the War of Independence and who was a witness to many of the events of the revolutionary period; my late mother, Kathleen, who also inspired me with a love of local history and regaled me with stories; my late father, Jim, who inspired my love of books.

My thanks to Paul and Ann Traynor for the photographs of the brothers Traynor; the Kildare Library and Arts Service, Newbridge, for the use of several of the photographs; Aisling Dermody, Blessington; Stan Hickey, Naas; Adhamhnan Ó Súilleabháin, Dublin; Dan O'Connor, Celbridge, for the donation of photographs; the late Paddy Sheehan, Newbridge, who was a mine of information on republican activity in Kildare; the late Marie Maher, Rathangan, who gave me the book of poetry by her uncle, Tom Behan; Liam Kenny, Naas, whose *Leinster Leader* articles have always been helpful; the late Lieutenant-Colonel Con Costello, Naas; Kenneth Ferguson of the *Irish Sword*; the late Enda Bracken, Naas; Michael Harris; Denis Fitzgerald and Brid Hoey; and last, but not least, my wife, Caroline, for her patience and perseverance.

INTRODUCTION

There were roughly 40,000 British troops and 10,000 armed police in Ireland during the War of Independence and yet a much smaller force of republicans managed to make the country ungovernable. County Kildare was an important axis for the republicans in intelligence gathering and for disrupting the communications of the British forces to the south and west. Nevertheless, until recently, the county received a bad press for its part in the war. There have been accusations that Kildare did not do as much as it could have. Indeed, due to the lack of military attacks and the low death toll attributable to revolutionary violence in the county, Kildare is rarely mentioned in any of the studies on the War of Independence. Michael Hopkinson, in *The Irish War of Independence*, wrote: 'Accounts of the conflict in these counties [Kildare, Carlow, Wicklow, Offaly and Laois] adopt an almost apologetic air as excuses are sought for their minimal involvement'.[1] Kildare's part in the War of Independence was virtually ignored until 2001, which saw the publication of my book *On the One Road. Political Unrest in Kildare 1913–1994*. Then, in 2006, an essay by Terence Dooley, 'IRA activity in Kildare during the War of Independence', focused on Kildare's part in the Anglo-Irish conflict, explaining the reasons why the county 'underperformed'.

The actions of County Kildare's inhabitants were no doubt heavily influenced by the positioning of four military centres in the county, with about one-third of Britain's overall military strength in Ireland based in the Curragh alone. The Kildare IRA was heavily outnumbered by crown forces and had neither the manpower nor weaponry to seriously challenge the military or police. About 300 activists in the county, with only about one-third of them ready to take to the field at any time, faced nearly 6,000 troops and hundreds of police and Black and Tans, coupled with a huge population of ex-servicemen and families tied to the military. There was unsurprisingly a fear of bringing retaliation for any attacks down on the Volunteers' communities. Indeed, the three main attacks that did occur in Kildare – at Greenhills, Maynooth and Barrowhouse – brought immediate reprisals from the forces of the crown. Moreover, the flat open plains of Kildare militated against ambushes, the Volunteers' favoured method of attack.

However, the situation in County Kildare was complex and its inhabitants were far from compliant. The county, with all its apparent obedience to the ruling power of the day, always had a reactionary element – be it the Maynooth men who walked the railway line to Dublin at Easter 1916; the many who participated in county-wide anti-conscription rallies, or the small band of dedicated Volunteers from Kill, Naas, Leixlip, Athy, etc. who took on the servants of the most powerful empire in the world. County Kildare was far from being a quiet backwater and its story during the War of Independence deserves to be reconsidered.

1

REPUBLICANISM AND NATIONALISM IN KILDARE 1795–1913

There have been many uprisings against the British presence in Ireland, but the 1798 rebellion was the first to have the establishment of a separatist republic as its goal. As the result of a combination of factors such as the Militia Act (a form of partial conscription) and the Convention Act (preventing unlawful general assemblies), organised political violence had become commonplace in County Kildare from the mid-1790s, while Defenderism was first publicly revealed in July 1795 with the arrest of two Defenders at Kilcock for attempting to swear a militiaman into their ranks. The Defenders were a militant, largely Catholic, secret organisation, formed in the 1780s to defend Catholics against arms raids by the Protestant Peep o' Day Boys. A mob of several hundred tried to rescue the two Defenders near Naas, but a strong military force deterred them. What alarmed the administration most was that one of the Defenders, Laurence

O'Connor, was a school teacher and not just an ordinary peasant. O'Connor was executed outside Naas Jail on 7 September 1795. When a branch of the Society of United Irishmen was formed in Kildare the Defenders provided them with a pool of organised radicals from which to recruit.

Political murders and attacks on property increased throughout Ireland during 1796–7 and on 30 March 1798, as attacks and acts of violence continued, a Privy Council proclamation declared Ireland to be in a state of rebellion and imposed martial law. Violence by the military and the use of 'free quarters' – the billeting of troops among the people – forced the 1798 leaders to push forward the date for the planned rebellion. This rash decision contributed to the defeat of the rebellion within a short period of time.[1]

In County Kildare the rebellion broke out on 24 May, with simultaneous attacks on Naas, Prosperous, Clane and Ballymore-Eustace.[2] The uprising soon engulfed the whole county, involving thousands of rebels in dozens of attacks and skirmishes. After some initial successes it evolved into a 'fugitive' war centred on the Bog of Allen, where rebels held government forces at bay for weeks. On 21 July William Aylmer surrendered his rebel army at Timahoe, effectively ending the rebellion in Kildare.[3] However, the rebellion's devastating effect on the county was felt for months to come as 'rebels and robbers' continued to raid and plunder. The situation was still dangerous in late 1798, but after January and February 1799 the number of alarming reports declined significantly.[4]

In response to the 1798 rebellion, the Act of Union of 1800 created the United Kingdom of Great Britain and Ireland, with 100 Irish MPs representing Ireland in the House of Commons at Westminster. The Act resulted in the abolition of the Irish parliament, which had existed in various forms since the thirteenth century, following England's conquest of most of Ireland in the twelfth century.[5] However, popular resistance to the British government and support for the United Irishmen continued to exist. After 1798 the United Irishmen had survived as an underground organisation and by 1800 a central executive had re-surfaced in Dublin. There was still much disaffection within the county and by late 1802 United Irish groups re-emerged.

The movement began to reorganise for a new rising and in County Kildare several thousand men, many of them veterans of 1798, attended meetings and secret drilling sessions. In July 1803 insurgents from Kildare converged on Dublin from the Naas and Celbridge directions for the planned uprising. The rebel leaders, Robert Emmet and Nicholas Gray, did not want any more than 300 Kildare men to come into the capital on the night of 22 July, so that the city would not look more crowded than usual. Some rebels from the Naas area began to make their way to the city as early as 20 July, but their leaders felt there were not enough arms or men from Dublin for the rising to be a success. Having had the disastrous experience of fighting with pikes against muskets in the unsuccessful attack on Naas in 1798, where they had suffered severe casualties, they were reluctant to make the same mistake again. As a result, many Kildaremen returned home again.[6]

Despite this, the rising went ahead in Dublin on the evening of 23 July. Failing to seize Dublin Castle, which was lightly defended, the rising amounted to a large-scale riot in the Thomas Street area. Robert Emmet soon lost control of his followers. In one incident, the Lord Chief Justice of Ireland, Arthur Wolfe

(Lord Kilwarden, of Forenaughts, Naas), was dragged from his carriage and piked to death. His nephew, Reverend Wolfe, who was travelling with him, was also killed as he tried to escape. Kilwarden's daughter, Marianne, escaped unharmed. Sporadic clashes continued into the night until finally quelled by the military at the estimated cost of forty dead, including several rebels from County Kildare.[7]

Although the rising in Dublin ended in failure, groups of rebels from many areas of Kildare were unaware of the fact. They continued to assemble in order to fulfil Emmet's plan and march on the capital. Maynooth was taken by a group of rebels, who then marched on Celbridge. A large number of insurgents assembled in Kildare town and Caragh, but by then they were all too late. A wave of arrests followed as the counties of Kildare and Meath were proclaimed.[8] The Lord Lieutenant, 3rd Earl of Hardwicke, commented after the July 1803 rebellion:

> I am sorry to say that such has been the state of the county of Kildare since the rebellion of 1798 as to require at all times the particular attention of government, and there is a more general and rooted spirit of disaffection in that county than any other part of Ireland.[9]

Martial law was imposed from 1803 to 1805 and an extensive manhunt for rebels was undertaken, with hundreds of arrests and imprisonments. When the government was satisfied that organised United Irish activity had finally been extinguished, the release of political prisoners commenced, but on 1 August 1807 the Insurrection Act was renewed.[10] This new Act, replacing the

1796 version, suspended trial by jury and implemented a penalty of seven years' transportation for breaking curfew, administering illegal oaths or possessing arms.

Catholics were disappointed. They had been anticipating a more liberal regime, Catholic Emancipation and the modicum of democracy they had been promised in return for the abolition of Ireland's Protestant-only parliament. Grim times lay ahead.

The situation in Kildare remained unsettled. There were raids by locals for arms in Athy and Naas; hidden arms were recovered by the military from thatched houses in the north of the county; an outright revolt was staged in Staplestown against the local militia; a raid to recover seized grain in Straffan led to a call for the reinforcement of the militia in Celbridge; in Kilcock, canal builders purposely breached the newly finished banks to try to get a few months' extra work to avoid starvation; an alleged rebellion was planned for 16 June 1814 in Kildare town according to the paranoid local magistrates; and in June 1820 Dubliners barricaded the Grand Canal after receiving false news of a rebellion in Kildare. Throughout the period *habeas corpus* (the legal requirement that a person under arrest should be brought before a judge or into court) was suspended, giving the Yeomanry (a volunteer cavalry force) effective powers of internment without trial.[11]

After nearly two decades of unrest, the crown's solution to the menace of Kildare was to build military barracks along the main road from Dublin to Cork and Limerick – at Naas in 1813, Newbridge in 1819, the Curragh in 1855 and Kildare town in 1901. Kildare soon became a garrison county tied to the British military presence economically through its trade and through the integration of the military with the civilian population. Naas Military Barracks became the depot of the Royal Dublin Fusiliers; Newbridge, a cavalry barracks; Kildare town, an artillery barracks; and the Curragh, the headquarters of the British Army in Ireland. Because of this military presence Kildare was a reasonably prosperous county even in times of economic hardship, particularly around its urban centres, and it also became a major recruiting area for the British Army.[12]

The large presence of crown forces in the urban areas throughout Ireland did not deter unrest in the countryside and in 1822 the Irish Constabulary Act established county police forces and a salaried magistracy.[13] Yet over the next twenty years agrarian secret societies continued their violent acts against British rule and the Protestant ascendancy. On 19 July 1823 the Tithe Composition Act was passed. This required all Irish citizens to pay monetary tithes to the Established Church – the Anglican Church in Ireland – instead of a percentage of agricultural yield. Roman Catholics – the majority of the population – resented this tax and an organised campaign of resistance to the payment resulted in large-scale refusals to pay. The campaign, which became known as the 'Tithe War', began on 3 March 1831 in Graiguenamanagh, County Kilkenny, when a force of 120 Yeomanry tried to enforce seizure orders on cattle belonging to a Roman Catholic priest. The 'war' continued until the tithe was abolished in 1838. Violence against Protestant churchmen and tithe proctors became an integral feature of the Tithe War and there were several killings of Protestants in County Kildare attributed to armed, secret societies such as the Whitefeet.[14]

At the same time a new leader, Daniel O'Connell, had emerged to lead the peasantry in its bid for Catholic Emancipation – the freedom to take part in government as officials, judges and members of parliament. O'Connell founded the Catholic Association in 1823, which became one of the most remarkable agencies of popular politicisation seen in Ireland. Catholic Emancipation was passed in 1829 and O'Connell then launched a campaign to repeal the Act of Union.[15] O'Connell and the Repeal Association held meetings in places as far apart as Baltinglass, Monaghan, Loughrea and Lismore, and in 1843 held a monster meeting at Mullaghmast, near Athy, where in 1578 English settlers had massacred dozens of local Irish chieftains. The members of the Repeal Association in County Kildare put a considerable amount of planning and work into arranging the Mullaghmast meeting. Local men from Athy, Ballitore and the surrounding areas were recruited to act as stewards and each man was given a hat badge which bore the inscription 'O'Connell's Police'. Thousands (reports vary from a possibly realistic 4,000 to an incredible 800,000) arrived to hear O'Connell say, 'Mullaghmast was selected for this meeting, as it was the spot on which English treachery and false Irish treachery consummated the massacre of the Irish people'. This meeting was to be the last monster meeting of the Repeal Association as O'Connell, in the face of possible military intervention, cancelled a later meeting planned for Clontarf.[16]

By the early 1840s County Kildare had settled down significantly and appeared reasonably prosperous. There had been considerable investment in the eighteenth century when many of its great houses (most notably Castletown House in Celbridge and Carton House in Maynooth) were built. The construction of the Grand Canal and the Royal Canal allowed for the transportation of goods from Dublin and throughout the county.[17] Despite its wealth, Kildare did not escape the disaster of the Great Famine, but it was spared its worst effects due to its relatively low population density. Kildare, with a population of 114,488 in the 1841 census, had an average total of 187 people per square mile of arable land in pre-Famine years. This was the lowest county figure in the country. Moreover, only 8.2 per cent of the arable land in the county was given over to the potato crop, compared with 28.5 per cent in Cork and 22.8 per cent in Mayo.[18] Nonetheless, the Famine hit some parts of the county severely and, as elsewhere, the poorer classes suffered most.

By the time the Great Famine ended, Ireland had lost over two-and-a-half million people out of a population of just over eight million. It is thought about one-and-a-half million people died of fever, starvation and cold during the years 1845–52, but the true figure will never be known. The last census before the Famine, taken in 1841, had been deficient in many respects, and part of the problem of distributing food in isolated areas during the Famine lay in the unexpected discovery of large numbers of people who had not been recorded before. No one could keep up with the numbers of people dying, so thousands died unknown and unmissed because their families had gone before them. Emigration accounted for the loss of another million people. The lowest population loss through death and emigration was in Leinster, the most prosperous province in Ireland – Kildare registered the third lowest loss, behind Louth and Wexford. Ulster came next, while Munster and Connaught lost between 23 and 28 per cent of their populations. The counties with the highest death rates were Sligo, Galway and Mayo, followed by Tipperary.[19]

Although its impact was not as severe as experienced in other counties, the Famine brought about major changes in Kildare society, most significantly the decline in population. Between 1841 and 1851 the county's population dropped by 16.39 per cent: from 114,488 to 95,723, a loss of 18,765. The decline continued, and by 1881 the population stood at 75,804. The only places where this trend did not manifest itself were the large towns of Naas and Newbridge, where the fall was negligible or where the population actually rose as people migrated from country areas. The siting of workhouses in Athy, Naas and Celbridge was also responsible for keeping the population levels up in the larger towns.[20]

The trauma of the Famine and the consequent readjustments provided an important impetus to the growth of political and cultural nationalism. Building on the foundations laid by the United Irishmen and Daniel O'Connell, a series of individuals and groups sought to cultivate a nationalist consciousness which was the precursor to new and distinctively Irish political and social arrangements.[21] The first of these bodies – known as the Young Ireland movement – led a failed uprising on 29 July 1848 in the village of Ballingarry, County Tipperary. After being chased by a force of Young Irelanders and their supporters, an Irish Constabulary unit raided a house and took those inside hostage. A gunfight of several hours followed, but the rebels fled after a large group of police reinforcements arrived.[22]

Some of the leaders of the Young Ireland movement who fled to America after the collapse of the insurrection formed clandestine organisations: Michael Doheny and John O'Mahony founded the Fenian Brotherhood in New York in 1855, while

James Stephens and Thomas Clarke Luby founded the Irish Republican Brotherhood (IRB). John Devoy, from Greenhills, Kill, was appointed by Stephens to take charge of promoting the Fenian organisation within the British Army in Ireland. Devoy had joined the French Foreign Legion when he was nineteen to gain military experience. He was posted to Algeria, but deserted a year later and returned to Ireland, joining the Fenian Brotherhood. He concentrated on the Dublin barracks and the Curragh Camp, recruiting hundreds of men into the organisation. Of the 26,000 regular troops stationed in Ireland, 60 per cent were Irish and it is estimated that 8,000 of these were Fenians. Of the militia force of 12,000, half were thought to be Fenians, while the army in England had some 7,000 men bound by the Fenian oath.

In 1865 the Fenians began preparing for a rebellion. Devoy based all his hopes of a successful insurrection on a mutiny in the British Army. He argued that lack of arms and trained men were the causes of past failures, but that there were many inadequately guarded arsenals and thousands of well-trained soldiers ready to change sides. The Fenians had about 6,000 firearms and as many as 50,000 men willing to fight. However, they delayed too long. In September 1865 the British moved to close down the Fenians' newspaper, the *Irish People*, and arrested much of the leadership, including Stephens and Luby. In 1866 *habeas corpus* was once again suspended in Ireland and there were hundreds of Fenian activists arrested, among them Devoy. The rising eventually took place in 1867, but it was an uncoordinated series of skirmishes which soon fizzled out: there was a brief rising in County Kerry in February; on 5 March other failed risings took place in Cork city, Limerick and Dublin. The largest of these engagements occurred at Tallaght, where several hundred Fenians clashed with the Irish Constabulary near the police barracks, but were driven off after a firefight. A total of twelve people were killed across the country on the day. When it became apparent that the planned co-ordinated rising had not transpired, most rebels simply went home.

Sentenced to fifteen years, John Devoy served five years until an amnesty in 1871 allowed him to leave for America.[23] Barred from returning to Ireland he travelled to Europe and conferred with Charles Stewart Parnell in Boulogne. (Parnell was elected MP for County Meath in 1875. He was active in the 'obstructionist' faction of the Home Rule Party, whose intention was to obstruct the day-to-day business of parliament to highlight Irish issues.)[24] Physical force republicans found common ground with constitutional nationalists committed to independence in a policy known as the New Departure: Devoy and Michael Davitt, for example, planned the Land League, which organised rent strikes and agitation on estates throughout the country. By 1880 the New Departure was in full swing: Parnell, Davitt and Devoy (in America) rallying Home Rulers, Land Leaguers and Fenians in a united camp.[25]

In the 1870s and 1880s demands for the recognition of Ireland's distinctive inheritance found practical political expression through the activities at Westminster of the Irish Parliamentary Party, under the leadership initially of Isaac Butt and subsequently Charles Stewart Parnell.[26] Both men sought to achieve a modest form of self-government known as Home Rule. Under it, Ireland would remain part of the United Kingdom, but would have limited self-government. The new Irish parliament would make decisions affecting Ireland's internal government, such as education, health and agriculture, while Westminster would still deal with external matters, such as trade and defence.

The Land League flourished in areas where the landlords were weak so, while there were many branches of the league in Kildare, they were not as strong as in other parts of the country because of the strength of the very large landlords such as the Duke of Leinster.[27] The weapon of the Land League was the 'Plan of Campaign', a device for collective bargaining on individual estates. Where landlords refused to lower the rent voluntarily, the tenants agreed to combine to offer a reduced rent. If the landlord refused to accept, the rent money would be lodged in an 'Estate Fund' used to support tenants evicted for adopting the 'Plan'. The Plan also called for 'land grabbers' to be boycotted. Traitors were to be expelled from the League and one such expulsion took place in Kildare, when a tenant on the O'Kelly estate in Clongorey was found to have paid his rent. Many condemned the Plan of Campaign, including Parnell and the Vatican.[28]

Fifty-one families were evicted from the O'Kelly estate in Clongorey between February 1883 and September 1892 for non-payment of rent. Relations between the landlord and the tenants had deteriorated rapidly after seizures of goods in lieu of rent, and the Land League became involved in negotiations to reduce rents. Six families were evicted in November 1888. The sub-sheriff, the estate agent and their emergency men – described as a 'sorry pack of corner-boy species' – were protected by 200 policemen and a company of the Black Watch Regiment from the Curragh. The *Leinster Leader* said, 'The soldiers with few exceptions did not relish their position.' The police, however, beat and cuffed men, women and children indiscriminately, and drove the people off from each eviction scene. Each emergency man was armed with a revolver and baton, while the police were in two bodies – one carrying rifles, the other armed with batons. In March 1889 twelve more families were evicted. This time the emergency men burned the homes to prevent their reoccupation. By May 1890 the whole area had been cleared.[29] Support for the evicted tenants came from a myriad of sources and forms, including the *Pall Mall Gazette*, which featured the plight of the tenants.[30]

Matthaus Maher, the principal trustee of the O'Kelly estate, had said he would rather see the land idle than negotiate with the Land League and his words became a reality: it lay unused for fourteen years. However, faced with mounting debts, unfarmed land and pressure from the trustees, Maher had to negotiate with representatives of the tenants to purchase their holdings.[31]

By the 1900s pressure for reform of the land system culminated in the Wyndham Act of 1903, which provided for long-term, low-interest government loans to buy out landlords' interests. The Act essentially transferred ownership from landlord to tenant and practically took the land issue out of the political equation.[32]

A number of Irish cultural organisations, set up in the late nineteenth century, grew in popularity in the early twentieth. They included the Gaelic Athletic Association (GAA) and the Gaelic League (Conradh na Gaeilge). Nationalistic Irishmen who believed that the spread of English games was undermining Ireland's identity formed the GAA in 1884. It developed as an openly nationalist organisation, excluding from membership those who watched or played 'foreign' games and all members of the British police or armed forces. From its creation the GAA attracted substantial support from the IRB, whose members saw it as a potential recruiting ground for nationalistic Irishmen. The growth of cultural nationalism reflected a growing interest in Ireland's past – its sport, language, mythology and folklore.

For political reasons the Royal Irish Constabulary (RIC) monitored GAA activities from its foundation. Michael Cusack, a teacher in Clongowes Wood College, Clane, was an organiser of the historic founding meeting of the GAA, so that village, un-surprisingly, had the first GAA club in County Kildare. At that time the link between the GAA and the nationalist movement was strong. It was the custom to name GAA clubs on national-istic and political lines, e.g. 'Sallins Robert Emmets' and 'Naas John Dillons'. By the turn of the century the rank and file GAA members were generally nationally minded and frequently mem-bers of the Gaelic League.[33]

When the Gaelic League was founded on 31 July 1893 it led to a great awakening of nationalism throughout Ireland. It was formed to restore Irish as a spoken and literary language. The founders regarded Irish as a vital repository of Ireland's culture and of the country's contribution to world civilisation. Its revival was also seen as a means of preserving Ireland's national identity and of 'de-Anglicising' the Irish people. Due to rapid social change the usage of Irish had declined sharply; before the Famine it was spoken by perhaps half of Ireland's population, but by the late nineteenth century it seemed in danger of becoming merely an academic subject.[34] By the first decade of the twentieth century the Gaelic League had successfully campaigned for compulsory teaching of the Irish language in schools and had established itself widely in urban areas. The Gaelic League was broad-based and, like the GAA, attracted Irish nationalists of different persuasions. Political advancement and cultural enrichment seemed to necessitate membership of both the GAA and Gaelic League.[35]

The political and land troubles of the late 1880s saw many nationalist provincial newspapers start up in opposition to Anglo-Irish papers such as *The Kildare Observer* – published in Naas in 1880 at 56 Market Square by the Grey family. The *Leinster Leader* was first published in Naas in mid-August 1880. The aim of its promoters was 'to strenuously and faithfully maintain the great principles of Irish nationality and liberal progress'. The paper was 'to reflect the true feelings of the people of the central counties of Ireland', as prior to this they had to content themselves with local newspapers bitterly opposed to popular aspirations. Some of the *Leader*'s chairmen came from the ranks of the local nationalist MPs, while many of its shareholders were parish priests and curates from Counties Kildare and Carlow. The *Leader*'s main competitors were the conservative *Kildare Observer* (Naas) and the *Leinster Express* (Portlaoise), but in 1883 a new nationalist paper entered the competition when P. J. Conlan, who had formerly worked on the staff of the *Leinster Leader*, set up his own newspaper at Carlow, the *Carlow Nationalist*, later known as *The Nationalist and Leinster Times*.

The first *Leinster Leader* company lasted only six years and was dissolved in 1886, when an agreement was reached with James Lawrence Carew, MP for North Kildare, whereby he took full control of the paper at a purchase price of £1,100. Carew held a strong influence over the paper up to the Parnell split in the Irish

Parliamentary Party. His career was at its height in the 1880s and he was jailed for supporting a boycott of evictors and land-grabbers.[36] However, he sided with Parnell and was eventually expelled from the Irish Parliamentary Party in 1900.

The *Leinster Leader* adopted a more impartial approach after Carew's death in 1903, but remained nationalist in outlook. Several factors intervened to ensure that no drift towards conservatism occurred. John Wyse Power, a member of the IRB, was the next editor. A founder member of the GAA, he was elected joint secretary of the national organisation and was one of its early leaders in Naas. Seumas O'Kelly, a playwright and author of distinction, became editor of the *Leader* in 1905. O'Kelly was the son of Michael O'Kelly of Loughrea, County Galway, who had been evicted from the Clanricarde estate in 1888. Seumas witnessed the evictions in his early years and they no doubt left a lasting impression on him. Under O'Kelly's editorship local news reports were increased, short stories were provided and extended coverage was given to Gaelic League events. O'Kelly founded a branch of the Gaelic League in Naas and brought the 'Theatre of Ireland' to the town to perform plays.[37]

In the political arena, nationalism suffered a series of set-backs in the late nineteenth century. The First Home Rule Bill was defeated in the House of Commons in 1886 and Parnell was deposed as leader of the Irish Parliamentary Party in 1890. He died the following year of a heart attack in his home in Dublin. Kildare was well-represented at Parnell's funeral – from town commissioners, clergy, businessmen, GAA clubs and Land League groups, to the Naas Labour Union, including a kinsman of the author, William Gaul of Rathasker Road, Naas.[38] In

September 1893 the Second Home Rule Bill was passed in the House of Commons, but defeated in the House of Lords.

At the time of the 1895 general election, the Irish Parliamentary Party was split, with the majority of its MPs following John Dillon (the 'Anti-Parnellites'), while a rump followed John Redmond (the 'Parnellites').[39] In the election County Kildare returned two anti-Parnellite MPs, prompting the *Leinster Leader* to declare: 'Kildare has reverted to Whiggery, not through the free unfettered choice of the electors, but owing to the ceaseless covert and insidious intimidation of [i.e. by] the clergy.' With only 5,007 people legally qualified to vote in the North Kildare constituency, Charles John Engledow, Irish National Federation, or Federationist, received 1,944 votes, while his rival James Lawrence Carew, Irish Party (IP), got 1,712 votes. However, 27 per cent of the electorate stayed away from the polls, possibly sick of the internecine strife or generally apathetic. In the South Kildare constituency, Matthew Minch was victorious for the Federationists.[40] A week after the election the *Leinster Leader* of 3 August 1895 lamented the loss of the Kildare constituencies:

The record of Kildare, one of the brightest in the history of Ireland, has been blotted by the name of Engledow. Kildare, the land of Lord Edward and Wolfe Tone [one of the founder members of the United Irishmen] the Saviour of the National cause in the days of danger and distress; Kildare that has always and ever disdained the policy of crawl; Kildare the pioneer of National freedom, has been betrayed and dishonoured by her enemies from within. Her birthright has been stolen from her by those who should be the guardians of her honour and integrity. *Quis custodiet custodes?* [Who will guard the guards?] They have betrayed their trust. They have foisted on the constituency whom? Oh, name him not – an unknown, an adventurer, a political tramp, here to-day and away to-morrow, a tool, who, when he has served the purpose of his employers, will be set aside without ceremony.

Social unrest continued in Kildare into the early twentieth century. Thirty years after the Great Famine, Kildare had become predominantly a pastoral and agricultural county devoted to the fattening of beef cattle and sheep production. It was a major region of cattle fattening because of its rich grasslands. The growth of ranches led to hostility between rancher and peasant, and Land League branches turned their attention to the practice of land-grabbing, the taking of untenanted pasture for short terms, usually eleven months. Auctions of untenanted pasture were frequently paralysed by the League's prohibition of such lettings, which contributed to rising rents. In addition, those who defied the ban – labelled 'grass grabbers' – were regularly subjected to rigorous boycotting and other reprisals by the League. At the same time, the ban brought graziers, who were active bidders for the landlords' pastures, into conflict with the League.

After the Land Act of 1903, antagonism between ranchers and peasants increased throughout the grazing regions, culminating in a campaign between 1906 and 1909 popularly termed 'the ranch war'. Public rallies and mass demonstrations became a regular feature of the anti-grazier agitation at which ranchers were regularly denounced. Graziers were also boycotted, although there is evidence that little boycotting took place in County Kildare. The most important tactic employed during the ranch war was cattle driving, in which animals were illegally removed from the grazier's land at night and taken to a secret market on the land of neighbouring farmers, or most often simply left to wander along country roads. Although cattle driving became the most popular method of operation, other forms of intimidation were used – the burning of hayricks, spiking meadows, destruction of turf, damaging of machinery, mutilation of horses and cows, and firing into dwelling houses.[41]

In the early twentieth century new, more nationalist, political forces also emerged. The commemoration of the centenary of the 1798 rebellion and the organisation of protest against the royal visits of Queen Victoria and Edward VII resulted in the formation of political pressure groups like the Dungannon Clubs. In September 1900 Dublin-born Arthur Griffith established an organisation called Cumann na nGaedheal – 'Society of Gaels' – to unite advanced nationalist/separatist groups and clubs. He had left school early to work as a printer before joining the Gaelic League. For a time he lived in Naas as his father was a compositor printer with *The Kildare Observer*. By advocating economic protectionism to develop Irish industry, Griffith looked forward to planning for an independent Ireland's future.[42]

In November 1905 Griffith founded Sinn Féin (SF) – 'Ourselves alone'. Éamon de Valera later said, 'Sinn Féin means literally "We ourselves." It was chosen as a motto of self-reliance.' Griffith had noted that Hungary won its independence by refusing to send members to the imperial parliament in Vienna, rejecting its claims to legislate for Hungary's internal affairs. He advocated a dual monarchy for Ireland, similar to that of Austro-Hungary, with separate legislatures for England and Ireland.[43] However, most Irish nationalists did not wish to see Ireland break all ties with Britain. These constitutional nationalists preferred to see Home Rule implemented. The Conservatives tried to kill the demand for Home Rule by making the Irish Party – now reunited under the leadership of John Redmond – more satisfied with government from Westminster, but the general election of 1910 left the Irish Party holding the balance of power (Liberals 275 seats, Conservatives 273). With seventy-one seats, the Irish Party could decide the future of the Liberal government. To stay in power, Herbert Asquith, the British Prime Minister, reluctantly did a deal with John Redmond – in return for the support of the Irish Party, the Liberals would introduce a Third Home Rule Bill. As a result of the Parliament Act of 1911, bills that passed the Commons in three consecutive sessions automatically became law. In 1912 Asquith succeeded in getting a Third Home Rule Bill passed by the House of Commons. The House of Lords vetoed it by 326 votes to 69. He reintroduced the Third Home Rule Bill again in January 1913. Again it passed through the Commons but the Lords imposed a two-year delay on its implementation. However, the Lords could not veto it a third time, so it was clear that the prospect of Home Rule for Ireland was now a reality.[44]

2

KILDARE RISING

In January 1913, when it became apparent that Home Rule would soon become a reality, the Ulster Volunteer Force (UVF) was formed from the numerous drilling parties which had been gathering at Orange Order halls to prepare for defence against its implementation. The UVF soon had around 100,000 members – headed by a distinguished array of retired British Army officers – who threatened to resist by physical force the implementation of Home Rule and the authority of any restored Dublin parliament by force of arms. Despite their avowed readiness to use force to prevent the implementation of Home Rule in Ulster, and their contingency plans for cutting communications and seizing arms and supplies from the crown forces, the UVF was left undisturbed.[1] The UVF served as a model for several paramilitary forces created by their nationalist political opponents.

From 26 August a major industrial dispute over the right to unionise industry began, which lasted until 18 January 1914. The dispute, which became known as the Dublin Lockout, was the culmination of a new generation of union leaders encouraging a more militant stance. The trade unions, led by men such as Jim Larkin and James Connolly, were pitted against the Dublin Federation of Employers and their figurehead, William Martin Murphy, who was determined, it seemed, to seek conflict rather than encourage the development of a joint conciliation board. Police attacks on demonstrations, most notably in Sackville (now O'Connell) Street, provoked the socialist James Connolly to call upon his fellow trade unionists to form a military force to protect workers in the dispute. This led to the formation of the Irish Citizen Army, a band of around 200 members who were mainly socialists and trade unionists.[2]

In late November 1913 the Irish Volunteers (Oglaigh na hÉireann) were formed in Dublin under the titular control of Eoin MacNeill, an historian prominent in the Gaelic League. They planned to help Britain enforce Home Rule whenever it passed and to oppose Ulster separatism.[3] Membership was open 'to all able-bodied Irishmen without distinction of creed, politics or social grade'. Unlike the Citizen Army, women were not allowed to join and were relegated to Cumann na mBan, an auxiliary body created the following April.[4]

Units of the Irish Volunteers were organised in nearly every parish in County Kildare during the early months of 1914. They were formed first in Naas, then Athy and Monasterevin.[5] The initial meeting to form a Volunteer Company in Naas was at a premises in Basin Street occupied by the County Agricultural Committee. A public meeting in the Assembly Room of the Town Hall followed, on 1 June 1914, but the room was unable to accommodate all the people who arrived. Considerable enthusiasm was aroused by speeches advocating a Volunteer corps and it was decided to make an immediate start. The gathering moved to the Town Hall yard where they were formed into companies. Drill instructors were selected and arrangements made for future drill exercises and other activities. Soon the Town Hall yard was inadequate for the numbers attending, so activity was switched to the unused jail.

The Volunteers procured caps and other equipment. They soon became more proficient in drill and they used wooden dummy guns as a substitute for rifles during drill exercises. The police, meanwhile, looked on helplessly, powerless to interfere in view of the numbers involved.[6]

Tensions began to rise and in an attempt to defuse the situation, Asquith tabled an amendment to the existing bill to allow the Ulster counties to remain outside the framework of Home Rule for a period of up to six years, during which time alternative solutions would be explored. Edward Carson, the unionist leader, rejected this outright, demanding that Ulster be 'given a resolution rather than a stay of execution'. This rebuff angered Asquith and over the next week plans were made to re-deploy troops from the Curragh Camp to Ulster in order to guard military installations and other strategic strong points. However, on 20 March 1914, in what is described as 'the mutiny at the Curragh', the Commander-in-Chief in Ireland, General Sir Arthur Paget, telegraphed the War Office that General Hubert Gough, an Ulsterman, and fifty-seven officers of the 3rd Cavalry Brigade offered to resign or accept dismissal rather than enforce Home Rule on Ulster.[7] In the subsequent confusion two senior general staff officers and the responsible minister were forced to resign, whereas the 'mutineers' were not punished – all they did was declare that they had offered to resign.[8] The government's attempts to intimidate Ulster unionists were subverted, but the effect of what happened when the general public found out had a profound influence on the future of Irish politics. To many it now seemed that the British government would compromise when faced with the threat of force.

In April 1914 – despite a ban on arms importation – the Ulster Volunteers, being worried that force would be used to impose Home Rule on the north-east, illegally imported 35,000 rifles from Germany. Nationalists were adamant that any partition was unacceptable and John Redmond declared that they could never assent to the mutilation of the Irish nation. In June 1914 the author and Irish nationalist Erskine Childers imported 900 German rifles for the Irish Volunteers on his yacht, *Asgard*.[9]

In Kildare the formation of the Irish Volunteers had created a major revival of nationalist feeling and in June 1914 companies of the new force were formed in Celbridge, Maynooth and Newbridge. On 7 June over 7,000 people gathered at the Gibbet Rath (where, in 1798, British troops had slaughtered over 300 rebels) on the Curragh, at 'the greatest Nationalist meeting seen for some time'. Companies of the Irish Volunteers from Maddenstown, Allen, Rathangan, Brownstown, Milltown, Nurney, Kilcullen, Ballymore-Eustace, Booleigh, Naas, Kildare and Newbridge, numbering around 1,000, paraded at the Stone Barracks. British troops quartered nearby, among them Dublin Fusiliers, were reluctant recipients of the loudly delivered patriotic speeches by Michael O'Rahilly and MPs for the county, John O'Connor and Denis Kilbride. Resolutions were adopted to form Volunteer corps in every town and district in the county, and to call for a repeal of the arms act to enable the people to arm for the defence of their country. In the same month another big parade of South Kildare Volunteers took place in the Agricultural Society enclosure in Athy. The Athy Battalion had four full companies, with a total complement of almost 1,000 Volunteers, a section of Cumann na mBan, a Fianna Éireann unit (Na Fianna Éireann was an organisation for young nationalist boys founded in 1909), and the distinction of having the only mounted troop in the country. By August the strength of the Volunteers in the county had increased to 6,000 and a County Kildare Committee for the Irish Volunteers was founded. The first meeting of this committee was held in the Town Hall, Naas, on 26 August. The attendance comprised representatives from most of the corps in the county.[10]

The increase in nationalist activity alarmed the British, but with the outbreak of war in Europe in the same month, the military's focus was directed towards preparation for combat. Home Rule was suspended until the war was over and in September John Redmond called on the Irish Volunteers to assist Britain by joining the British Army, a proposal rejected by militant nationalists. The Irish Volunteers split, with the majority following Redmond and becoming known as the National Volunteers. The minority, dominated by the IRB, kept the title of Irish Volunteers and began preparing for an insurrection while Britain was fighting in Europe. Only five Kildare companies: Naas, Maynooth, Kill, Prosperous and Athgarvan remained loyal to the Irish Volunteers. The auxiliary organisations, Cumann na mBan and Fianna Éireann, largely supported the dissidents. Following the split, British Intelligence believed the number of Irish Volunteers in Kildare to be 344, armed with twenty-four rifles.[11]

One of the members was Michael O'Kelly. In 1912 Seumas O'Kelly had resigned as editor of the *Leinster Leader* to accept the editorship of the *Saturday Evening Post* in Dublin. His more militant brother, Michael, succeeded him. Michael O'Kelly's strong nationalist views were reflected in the *Leader*, especially in reports concerning the British Army and its war effort, which were considerably muted compared with those of the pro-British *Kildare Observer*. A serious clash of views occurred in October 1914 when Michael O'Kelly wrote a long editorial on 'Ireland and the war' in which he attacked 'the unholy lust of capitalists and others' and argued that Ireland's quarrel was with Britain and not Germany. Yet over the next two years the editor generally quoted the opinions of others on the main issues of the day, without committing the *Leader* to any particular policy.[12] By then he was a member of Naas Company, Irish Volunteers, and perhaps thought it wise not to draw attention to this fact.

In the autumn of 1915 Dr Ted O'Kelly from Maynooth was appointed by the Irish Volunteers' GHQ in Dublin as organiser of the Volunteers in Kildare. In September a conference of delegates from the various units in north Kildare was held at the house of Michael O'Kelly, the *Leinster Leader* editor. The meeting was attended by Ted O'Kelly, Maynooth; Michael O'Kelly, Naas; Patrick Dunne, Kill; Domhnall Ua Buachalla, Maynooth; Thomas Harris, Prosperous; Arthur James Kickham (Art) O'Connor, Celbridge; and Michael Smyth and Éamon Ó Modhrain, Athgarvan. Arrangements were made to reorganise the Volunteers locally and those present were appointed as an organising committee for north Kildare. Smyth and Ó Modhrain were asked to help extend the organisation in south Kildare as there was no unit of the Volunteers in that area. At that time there were only five companies in County Kildare – Naas, Kill, Maynooth, Prosperous and Athgarvan, all in the north and middle of the county. Those present at the meeting were appointed to attend a conference with the National Executive of the Irish Volunteers on 25 October, where a number of matters were discussed – improved organisation, training and arming of units, etc. Towards the end of the year Volunteer manoeuvres were held between Naas and Newbridge and Naas and Athgarvan Companies, under Lieutenant Ted O'Kelly. At this time a few Volunteers bought pistols and ammunition, which were kept in the home of Michael O'Kelly.[13]

As the war in Europe progressed, invalided soldiers returned home and were recruited by the Volunteers as training officers. One such man was William Jones, who as a reservist had drilled the Volunteers before he was called up for active service with the Connaught Rangers. Wounded and shipped home after service in France, he again joined the Athgarvan Company and acted as training instructor. Jones was employed in the Curragh Camp, but after an argument with some fellow workers he was arrested in September 1915 under the Defence of the Realm Act (DORA). This, the first in a series of emergency Acts to give the British forces and police wide-ranging powers to arrest suspected traitors, was passed in November 1914, partly to prevent collaboration between Irish separatists and Germany. Jones lost his job in the camp and his army pension. Ex-Corporal Jones was sentenced at Lumville court to three months' imprisonment, which was afterwards altered to a fine of £5 owing to his army service. He set about training the Volunteers with enthusiasm, instructing them in drill, rifle and revolver practices in the local Gaelic Hall, and field exercises, which were carried out on the Curragh, only a few hundred yards from the camp. In January 1916, at revolver practice, Thomas Wilmot was severely wounded accidentally. He was brought as a patient to the Drogheda Memorial Hospital, but the whole incident was hushed up as Dr Laurence Rowan, Kildare, who was medical officer for the local Volunteers, attended to Wilmot's wound.[14]

Training for a rebellion continued in other parts of the county and a 'bomb factory' was set up at St Catherine's in Leixlip. Tins of gunpowder, detonators, safety fuses, cartridges, milk cans and scrap iron, some of which were made into bombs, were discovered in a raid there in 1915.[15] In Maynooth, shopkeeper Domhnall Ua Buachalla began preparing his small company for a rebellion and had pikes made to deal with British cavalry in the event of street fighting. (The pikes were later sent to Dublin and used in the Easter Rising.) He also bought around twenty-four shotguns and stored them in the attic, where they lay undiscovered during police raids.[16] As the Athgarvan Company was the nearest to the Curragh Camp, it was given the task of procuring arms and ammunition from the soldiers based there. Good supplies of 1915 pattern Lee-Enfield rifles were acquired, mainly from English soldiers, with money provided by GHQ. Sympathetic civilian workers on the Curragh firing ranges provided the ammunition. Eventually locked rifle-racks were placed in the army billets, ending the trade. The Athgarvan Company also purchased 100 Martini-Enfield rifles from the National Volunteers, with £300 provided by GHQ. At that time British Intelligence believed the Irish Volunteers in the county had 111 rifles, while there were still 209 weapons in the possession of the National Volunteers.[17]

In America John Devoy had become head of the Irish republican movement there. Its chief organisation was Clan na Gael
(Family of the Irish). Devoy lived in New York and had important
allies among the Irish-American community. Following his arrival
in America after expulsion from Ireland in 1871, Devoy brought
unity to the various Irish-American organisations, which were in
disarray after the failed Fenian invasion of Canada. He worked
tirelessly for the cause of Irish freedom and in his offices at *The
Gaelic American* wrote letters and articles and stoked in every
way possible his hatred for England. He assisted in fund-raising
efforts for the Irish Volunteers and other Irish organisations, and
negotiated for arms from Germany for the 1916 Rising.

When the labour leader Jim Larkin went to America at the
end of 1914, he took with him a letter of introduction from
Tom Clarke, an old friend of Devoy's from his Fenian days.
While America had not yet entered the war, it was economically
supportive of the British war effort. Larkin saw it as his duty to
support labour disputes that would disrupt this support. Devoy
saw it as his duty to support anyone who was in conflict with
British interests, including Germany. Thirty years previously
Devoy had prophesied in a speech in Holyoke, Massachusetts:
'Ireland's opportunity will come when England is engaged in a
desperate struggle with some great European power or European
combination'. He brought Larkin into contact with the German
military attaché and while Larkin refused outright to help the
German war effort, he did accept financial assistance towards
labour disputes, which was channelled to him via Devoy.

In Germany Sir Roger Casement, an Antrim-born patriot,
was attempting to form an Irish Brigade among Irish prisoners

of war. His attempts met with little success. Only fifty-two men joined and German promises to give these men instruction in the use of machine guns were not kept. Casement had hoped for a great German expedition to Ireland with German officers, submarines and at least 200,000 rifles, plus machine guns for the use of his brigade. The knowledge that only a cargo of 20,000 rifles and ammunition was to be sent, reduced the already ill Casement to despair. He didn't realise that Devoy and Clan na Gael, on behalf of the IRB, had accepted this offer and counted on nothing more, or that a landing of Germans, other than a few officers, was not asked for or desired by the leaders of the Rising at home.[18]

Despite the failure of Casement's Irish Brigade, plans for a rebellion continued and in early 1916 a meeting was held in Michael O'Kelly's home at Gleann na Greine, Naas, to prepare for local action. Present were Tom Harris, Prosperous; Domhnall Ua Buachalla and Patrick Colgan, Maynooth; and Michael Smyth, Athgarvan. Ted O'Kelly informed Michael O'Kelly on Ash Wednesday that a rising was to occur on Easter Monday and he was to inform his members. Instructions had been received from Volunteer GHQ that the Kildare units were to be 'used as outpost groups between the Curragh Camp and Dublin when the outbreak took place'. Kildare Volunteers had been assigned the crucial task of preventing British troops from the Curragh reaching Dublin. The RIC barracks at Sallins and Kill were to be attacked, but as there were only five understrength companies in the area that plan was abandoned. GHQ expected the Kildare Volunteers to provide 100–150 men to demolish railway lines, roads and other communications (telegraph and telephone wires) between Dublin and the Curragh. The main plan was to destroy the railway bridge over the canal outside Sallins to prevent troops from the Curragh getting to Dublin. Once these objectives were completed the Kildare Volunteers were to march to Dublin to join the rebels. On Wednesday 19 April Tom Byrne, an ex-soldier with military experience from the South African (Boer) War, brought news to Naas from headquarters in Dublin that a nationwide rising was to take place on Sunday 23 April at 6 p.m.[19]

On the night of Good Friday, 21 April, the Athgarvan Company was mobilised. The sixteen men who turned out were told to stand by for a call-out on Sunday and in the meantime to go to confession and Holy Communion. The next day Michael Smyth learned of a split in the Executive Committee of the Volunteers, but decided to obey the mobilisation orders he had received. However, the 'manoeuvres' were unexpectedly cancelled by an announcement signed by Eoin MacNeill on Saturday night, 22 April, and published in the Sunday newspapers the following morning:

> Owing to very critical position, all orders given to Irish Volunteers for tomorrow morning, Easter Sunday, are hereby rescinded, and no parades, marches, or other movements of Irish Volunteers will take place. Each individual Volunteer will obey this order strictly in every particular.[20]

On Easter Sunday morning the sixteen members of the Athgarvan Company paraded, but stood down when they received the countermanding orders from Dublin. They paraded again on Monday, but when no further orders were forthcoming, they again stood down.[21]

In Naas confusion arose when the Rising was reportedly called off on Easter Sunday. Ted O'Kelly, Thomas Harris and Michael O'Kelly had a meeting and later received a dispatch, which confirmed that the Rising was to take place. All returned to Michael O'Kelly's home, collected their pistols and ammunition and left on their bicycles to inform their comrades. Rendezvous was to be at Bodenstown and they were to destroy the railway bridge over the canal to prevent reinforcements reaching Dublin as planned. Michael O'Kelly saw Tommy Patterson and Tommy Traynor, both of Naas Company and asked them to be in Bodenstown. He records in his witness statement that:

Having waited there [Bodenstown] for some time, I concluded that something went amiss with the arrangements. Returning to Sallins, I met T. Patterson and T. Traynor [Patterson and Traynor had mobilised with their companies, but owing to the confusion did not travel to Bodenstown], and they were both very much disappointed when I informed them that I failed to see anybody at the meeting place ... On our return to Naas we heard of the failure of the train service, but it was not until the evening was well advanced that it became generally known that a revolutionary outbreak had occurred in Dublin, and that this was the cause of the non-arrival of the railway trains as usual. Next day I saw T. Patterson again, and he was still very much upset and expressed his determination to try and reach Dublin. I tried to persuade him from this purpose, pointing out that it was desirable that some local assistance should be available for guiding and supplying information to the Republican forces, should the fighting spread to Naas. In this connection I recall that he had made a sketch, or plan, showing the main approaches to the town, and also places in the town itself where implements useful for barricading, erecting defence works, etc., could be procured. I prevailed with him at length but as more news of the fighting in Dublin arrived, he again became anxious and desirous to make an attempt to reach Dublin. As the day wore on the activities of the R.I.C. increased, and each of us was in turn questioned as to our movements on Monday.[22]

Captain Patrick Dunne, OC Kill Company, received word on Easter Sunday night from Michael O'Kelly that he was to rendezvous with Tom Byrne and Ted O'Kelly at Bodenstown on Easter Monday at 11.30 a.m. Eight men of the Kill Company mobilised and were armed and awaiting instructions that night. Why Captain Dunne did not go to Bodenstown, as ordered, is unclear. However, on Easter Monday evening Tommy Patterson and Tommy Traynor arrived in Kill and reported that Michael O'Kelly had waited in Bodenstown for over two hours and that Tom Byrne and Ted O'Kelly did not turn up. Minutes after Michael O'Kelly left, Tom Harris, Ted O'Kelly and Tom Byrne arrived, and after a time, proceeded to Maynooth. Michael O'Kelly had, by then, returned to Naas. On Tuesday of Easter Week Captain Dunne decided to send Father O'Brien, CC, Kill Parish, who was a member of the local company, to try to reach Dublin for instructions. By Thursday Fr O'Brien had not returned so Dunne decided to demobilise his men that evening.[23]

On Wednesday some men arrived in Naas from neighbouring areas; they had also been notified about the meeting at Bodenstown, but for reasons unclear failed to turn up. There is general confusion in the witness statements about the failure to mobilise in Bodenstown, with some participants placing the blame on

Éamon Ó Modhrain, who travelled around the county countermanding the Rising orders. It was later learned that Tom Harris,
Tom Byrne and Ted O'Kelly had assembled in Bodenstown, but
when no other Volunteers arrived, the plot to destroy the bridge
was abandoned and the party went on to Maynooth. They joined
the Maynooth Volunteers who were on their way to Dublin. The
core of the Maynooth Company had mobilised on Monday at
3 p.m. after getting word of the Rising: its OC, Domhnall Ua
Buachalla, led a thirteen-man contingent on a march from Maynooth to Dublin to take part in the fighting. On Tuesday morning of Easter Week the fourteen Kildare men marched in formation into the city and when they came in sight of the General
Post Office (GPO) in Sackville Street there was a great cheer, as
the men there had been expecting them. Rebel leaders Patrick
Pearse and James Connolly greeted them at the door. They were
given tea, eggs and cigars and, according to Tom Harris from
Prosperous, were addressed by Connolly, who said, 'It didn't matter a damn if we were wiped out now as we had justified ourselves.'[24] Patrick Colgan from Maynooth recalled: 'We entered
the GPO by the main entrance. Commandant General Connolly
was at the door. As we entered he shook each of us by the hand
and smiled his welcome to us. Connolly was one of my heroes. I
had never before met him. I felt all excited that he would show
such an interest in us.'[25] The fourteen men who had walked from
Maynooth were delighted to see at least six more Kildare men in
the GPO garrison, including Frank Bourke of Carbury and Jim
O'Neill from Leixlip.[26]

In Dublin the Irish Volunteers and the Irish Citizen Army
began the Easter Rising at noon on Easter Monday, 24 April,

when they commandeered dozens of buildings and positions throughout the city. Eoin MacNeill's countermanding order caused as much confusion there as in the countryside and only around 1,600 men, women and children mobilised for action. A contingent of Volunteers and Citizen Army men formed up at the Irish Transport and General Workers' Union (ITGWU) headquarters at Liberty Hall and marched up the quays to the GPO, on Dublin's main thoroughfare. James Connolly gave the order to charge the building. From the steps of the commandeered GPO, President of the Provisional Government Patrick Pearse read the Proclamation that he had helped compose, announcing that the rebels were setting up a provisional government replacing the British government.[27] Frank Bourke recalled:

> Shortly after our arrival the tricolour was hoisted on the flagstaff at the left-hand corner facing Prince's Street. Commandant Pearse read aloud to the public on the street the Proclamation of the Irish Republic and copies of the Proclamation were posted on the walls and pillars of the building.[28]

The Maynooth Volunteers fought in the GPO and in outlying defensive posts at Parliament Street. Jim O'Neill, Citizen Army, was in the GPO as Quartermaster General in charge of munitions, while Frank Bourke was part of the small group of teachers and pupils from St Enda's styling themselves 'Pearse's Own'. Tom Harris was wounded by 'friendly fire' in the GPO, while Major Alfred E. Warmington of Naas, serving with the 10th Royal Irish Regiment, was one of the first fatal casualties of the Rising. He was killed in action on Easter Monday in the fighting in the

South Dublin Union. As British reinforcements rushed into the city on the first day of the Rising, Private James Duffy, 3rd Royal Irish Regiment, from Carrisvilla, County Kildare, was mortally wounded. Another Kildare native, George Geoghegan, was killed in the fighting at Dublin Castle. Geoghegan (35) was a married man with three children. Born at the Curragh, he lived on Cork Street, Dublin, was employed at the Inchicore Railway Works and was a bandsman in the Citizen Army.[29]

For the Kildare men in the GPO garrison, one of the most thrilling episodes of the week occurred just before the evacuation on Friday, when the Volunteers present burst into the 'Soldier's Song', their voices rising above the roar of the encircling inferno. It was a hopeless fight, but here was an expression of defiance against the might of British power and of faith that from the ashes of the doomed GPO would rise the independent Ireland for which they had fought.

Violent street fighting continued until the afternoon of 29 April when Pearse offered to surrender his forces to spare the people of Dublin further bloodshed. At 3.30 p.m. Pearse met Brigadier-General Lowe at the top of Moore Street. Captain Henry Eliardo de Courcy Wheeler of Robertstown, County Kildare, who was serving at the Curragh with the Army Service Corps, accompanied Lowe. Pearse was driven to a meeting with General John Maxwell, the newly arrived British Commander-in-Chief, where he signed the surrender document. Captain Wheeler accompanied Elizabeth O'Farrell, a courier and nurse for the GPO garrison, to Moore Street with Pearse's order to surrender.[30] Some of the men wanted to fight on, but Tom Clarke and Seán MacDermott persuaded them that they would have another day. It was then agreed that the wounded James Connolly be moved to the hospital at Dublin Castle and stretcher-bearers took him through the British barricades.[31]

The Easter Rising was effectively over. Around 450 people died in the week-long fighting: eighty rebels, including fifteen who were executed, 132 military and police, and around 240 civilians. Damage to property amounted to around £2.5 million, a huge sum at the time.[32] *The Kildare Observer* carried several editorials condemning the Rising, while those of the *Leinster Leader* and the *Nationalist* were more sympathetic. On 2 May 1916 the *Observer* printed an edition of the paper devoted to the Rising in which a special correspondent reported:

All other means of transport being denied me I set forth for Dublin from Naas on Sunday morning, having seen the telegram from the Castle to the Naas police confirming the reported surrender of the rebels. I was informed under these circumstances that I should very probably require no passport to enable me to enter the city, and therefore did not even take the precaution of bringing documents that would prove my identity to the satisfaction of anyone challenging my bona-fides. En route I met many cyclists and pedestrians coming from the direction of the city but none seemed to know anything definite about the situation there. I first questioned a couple of cyclists near Clondalkin. They told me that the fighting was still 'terrible'.

The reporter ventured into the city and was given a pass by the military at a checkpoint at Dolphin's Barn. He visited most of the battle sites and reported that snipers were still firing at the military. The *Observer* editorials took a pro-British stance and expressed outrage at the betrayal of the soldiers at the Front and at the disruption of trade and commerce.[33] The *Leinster Leader*'s attitude to the rebellion was at first one of horror, but this soon turned to sympathy. The *Leader* placed the blame for the Rising on the unionists in the north who had spurned constitutional methods. However, the editor, Michael O'Kelly, was not responsible for the critical editorials, as both he and two other members of staff had been arrested in the first week of May by the RIC in Naas. Seumus O'Kelly, who had returned to Naas because of ill-health, temporarily assumed editorship of the *Leader*.[34]

Michael O'Kelly was arrested with his nephew, Alfie Sweeney, and taken to the local RIC barracks, then to military prison at Hare Park, in the Curragh and subsequently to Richmond Barracks in Dublin. Michael was deported to Wakefield, while Alfie Sweeney was released, being only sixteen. When O'Kelly and Sweeney were taken to Naas RIC Barracks they found that other arrests had already been made in the town. The men arrested were Paddy Grehan, South Main Street; Christy Byrne, Tower View; Dick Furlong, Killashee; Pat Mooney, Millbrook Villas; and T. J. Williams, a reporter on the *Leinster Leader*. (Williams was released after being in custody for a day.) Another sixteen men picked up in various parts of the county joined the Naas prisoners in the Curragh. They were all brought to Dublin's Richmond Barracks under military escort.[35]

There was very little sympathy with the rebels. In the chambers of Kildare County Council, Mr John Healy proposed the following resolution:

That we, the members of the Kildare Co. Council, strongly deprecate the recent deplorable action of a section of our countrymen in resorting to force of arms. At the same time we strongly appeal in what we consider the best interests of this country and the Empire as a whole to the Government to extend the greatest possible clemency to the rank and file, who, we believe, were deceived into taking part in the rising. That we take this opportunity of again recording our unabated confidence in Mr. J. E. Redmond and the Irish Parliamentary Party, and thoroughly endorse the attitude they adopted during the crisis we are passing through.[36]

General Sir John Maxwell was appointed supreme military governor and given *carte blanche* to deal with the aftermath of the Rising. He determined that it was an act of treason in a time of war. Maxwell oversaw the mass arrests of republican suspects and the court-martialling of 183 people, ninety of whom received the death sentence for their part in the Rising, with Maxwell overseeing all the trials.[37] Between 3 May and 12 May fifteen rebel leaders were shot, including the seven who had signed the Proclamation – Patrick Pearse, James Connolly, Tom Clarke, Éamonn Ceannt, Seán MacDermott, Thomas MacDonagh and Joseph Plunkett. The first executions took place quickly – only two days after the last rebel surrender – and then were dragged out over ten days, which had a powerful effect on public opinion. The execution of the leaders of the Rising produced more sympathy in the country than the actual events themselves and slowed down recruitment to the British Army. Anger was turned increasingly towards the British and sympathy and support for the rebels grew: for most nationalists, Home Rule was no longer enough. Sinn Féin stood for independence from Britain and the general public flocked to support them.

On 21 May 1916 General Maxwell visited Maynooth College. After the executions he was universally hated and constantly referred to as 'The Butcher' or 'Bloody Maxwell'. He was visiting the college to reprimand the president for giving his blessing to the men of Maynooth as they set forth for Dublin on Easter Monday. He had previously called on Dr Walsh, Archbishop of Dublin, asking him to punish priests for attending wounded and dying rebels. Dr Walsh, a conscientious priest, quickly reprimanded Maxwell for his interference in the most sacred duty of the priest and refused to take any orders in the matter. Maxwell's reception party in Maynooth was small and his visit short. He was angrily informed that his interference was not acceptable. A student in Maynooth at the time wrote:

> Shortly after the Rising when his blood-thirsty task had been completed, Sir John Maxwell, accompanied by some of his staff visited Maynooth for the alleged purpose of telling the Bishops and the college authorities where their duty lay. The fall of a pin would have sounded like a cannon-shot in the icy, hostile silence with which the students greeted the party. It was an experience which the ex-Jameson Raider was not likely to forget.[38]

The change in public opinion was soon recognised by the British. No more executions took place after the wounded James Connolly was taken by stretcher and executed by firing squad in a chair in Kilmainham Jail on 12 May.[39]

3

WHO FEARS TO SPEAK OF EASTER WEEK?

In the days immediately after the Easter Rising, 3,149 men and seventy-seven women were arrested throughout the country. In their panic the authorities rounded up national figures, republicans and general dissidents. These prisoners were held in Richmond Barracks in Inchicore, which was close to the British General Headquarters in the Royal Hospital, Kilmainham. The first prisoners arrived in Richmond Barracks on 30 April and the first group was deported to England that night. The leaders of the Rising were court-martialled in a separate building and those sentenced to death were brought to Kilmainham Jail. Around 160 people were convicted by court-martial while 1,852 men and five women were interned without trial. These internees were transferred to prisons in England.[1]

Oliver O'Ryan (Maynooth) and Jim O'Neill (Glasnevin and Leixlip) were among 200 prisoners transferred to Knutsford on 1 May. Another 289 went to Stafford Detention Barracks on the same day, including Michael Cosgrove, Castleknock, with a home address of Coolridge, Kilcock; Frank Bourke, Hermitage, Rathfarnham, Dublin, with a home address of Carbury; and Tim Tyrell and Pat Kirwan, Maynooth. Two days later another 308 went to Knutsford, including Domhnall Ua Buachalla, Maynooth. On 6 May 376 were transferred to Wakefield Detention Barracks, among them boatmen Andrew and James Dunne from Allenwood. On 8 May Pat Colgan of Maynooth went with 202 others to Stafford. On 15 May three Maynooth men were court-martialled and sentenced to two years (eighteen months remitted). They were John Greaves, Joseph Ledwich and Patrick Weafer. Twelve Kildare men were among the 273 prisoners sent to Wakefield a week later.[2]

Most of the Irish prisoners were sent to England by cattle boat and while their military guards were given life belts, in case of being torpedoed by German U-boats, the prisoners received none.[3] The prisoners were denied formal prisoner-of-war status, but in a classic British solution were treated like prisoners of war. In June 650 internees were released, among them Ed Cosgrove (Newbridge), Dr Laurence Rowan, Alfie Sweeney, Andrew and James Dunne, Nicholas and Chris Byrne, Jack Fitzgerald, Louis Moran, Michael O'Kelly, Pat Mooney and Pat Grehan.

The most influential prisoners, including Arthur Griffith, were sent to Reading Jail. Those whose death sentences were commuted to life imprisonment, such as Éamon de Valera, Countess Markievicz, William Cosgrave and Tom Ashe (who led his battalion in the Battle of Ashbourne during Easter Week), were sent to convict prisons in England. Eoin MacNeill, whose countermanding order had crippled the Rising, declared himself responsible with the other leaders and was sentenced to penal servitude for life. He was sent to Dartmoor Prison, where he was welcomed by de Valera and afforded the respect of his rank as Chief of Staff by the Volunteers. The remaining prisoners were sent to Frongoch Camp in Merionethshire, North Wales, a former internment camp for German prisoners. Gaelic games were organised to boost morale and maintain fitness.[4]

In Frongoch, an effort to conscript some of the internees into the British Army was resisted by all prisoners. There were around sixty men in Frongoch who had lived in Britain before the Rising and they were accordingly deemed liable for conscription, but the prisoners refused to co-operate and combined to make identification of those men impossible. In retaliation the prisoners were confined to their huts and some were sentenced to terms of hard labour. A forty-eight-hour hunger strike by 200 prisoners, regained them their lost privileges.[5]

Domhnall Ua Buachalla was one of the most prominent prisoners in Frongoch. He was on the General Council, or 'Civil Government of the Irish Republic in Frongoch' as they styled themselves. (Ua Buachalla was also a member of a shadowy group in the camp called 'The Black Hand'.) However, the General Council did not last long and a Military Council soon replaced it as the IRB reorganised and extended its influence.

With the establishment of a Military Council, Frongoch provided an ideal opportunity for the republican movement to develop the philosophy of revolution and it became known as 'the University of Revolution'. It set the pattern for Irish republican prisoners in many subsequent periods of internment throughout the remainder of the twentieth century. Military matters began as soon as all fatigue duties were finished. Military science was taught from smuggled-in manuals, military discipline was learned and the advantages of guerrilla warfare in a future conflict were taught. Irish language and history were also taught. When the prisoners eventually returned to Ireland everyone would have a part to play. Specialist skills were passed on to other internees and experienced men would be sent to parts of the country where Sinn Féin and the IRA were at their weakest.

The first major mistake the British made in 1916 was executing the leaders of the Rising. Their second mistake, and by far their biggest blunder, was putting the majority of the men of Easter Week in the same camp, for the internees of Frongoch, including Michael Collins, Richard Mulcahy, Dick McKee, Tomás MacCurtain, Terence MacSweeney, Seán T. O'Kelly, Oscar Traynor and Seán Russell, became the leaders in the War of Independence.[6]

There were seventeen prisoners from County Kildare in Frongoch. Several Kildare men, who resided in Dublin, fought with the Dublin Brigade or the Citizen Army and are listed with the contingent from the capital, which at 926, was the highest. The men listed for Kildare were:

Michael Smyth, Athgarvan
James Corrigan, Ballitore
William Corrigan, Ballitore
Edward Moran, Ballysax
Michael Cosgrove, Kilcock
James O'Neill, Leixlip
Patrick Colgan, Maynooth
John Kenny, Maynooth

Pat Kirwan, Maynooth

John Maguire, Maynooth

Thomas Maguire, Maynooth

Thomas Mangan, Maynooth

Liam O'Reagain, Maynooth

Oliver O'Ryan, Maynooth

Tim Tyrell, Maynooth

Domhnall Ua Buachalla, Maynooth

Tom Harris, Prosperous[7]

Frongoch was divided into two camps: the south camp, which contained a former distillery that was divided into dormitories, and several other huts and buildings; and the north camp, which contained thirty-five wooden huts in two rows. The men in the distillery were housed in the grain lofts, which were infested with rats. The rows of huts in the north camp were christened Pearse and Connolly after the executed leaders. The two camps were surrounded by barbed wire and guarded by armed British troops, though these were mainly soldiers too old for service at the Front.

The Irish situation was becoming an increasing embarrassment to the British government. Some of the less militant prisoners were released and by the end of July only 600 men remained at Frongoch. On 11 July a group of thirty men, including most of the leadership, was transferred to Reading Jail. The British felt that their removal would make the men in Frongoch easier to control. They were wrong. J. J. 'Ginger' O'Connell was replaced as commandant of the south camp by Michael Staines, while Eamonn Morkan, Kildare, replaced M. W. O'Reilly as commandant of the north camp. Morkan was an employee of the

National Bank and, though originally from Kildare, lived at 49 Whitworth Road, Dublin.

On 3 November another group of leaders was transferred to Reading Jail, among them Eamonn Morkan. Each time the British removed the leaders a new crop came forward to replace them. This was indicative of the depth of talent in Frongoch. The experience of prison greatly benefited the republican movement. It provided a meeting place for a large number of republicans who shared the same ideas and goals. It also allowed friendships to develop and ideas to be exchanged. Patrick Colgan conversed with Michael Collins when they were both in Frongoch and on their release Collins turned to Colgan to organise north Kildare.[8]

Revelations about the poor fare, appalling living conditions and harsh administration in Frongoch dominated the home news, firing up previously dormant nationalists. Naas Urban District Council (UDC) sent this letter of protest to the British government:

> That we, the elected public representative bodies of the County Kildare, beg respectfully to bring before His Majesty's Government the continued imprisonment at Frongoch of several persons from this county without trial, and without any specific charge having being brought against them, arising out of the rebellion which occurred last April. That having regard to the peaceful condition of the County and that no overt act was committed therein during the rebellion, we regard the continued imprisonment of these men, as entirely unjustified, and opposed to British conceptions of Justice, and on these grounds, and for the sake of furtherance of the mutual good relations existing between the Irish and British peoples, we pray for the immediate

release of these men who have already suffered seven months' rigorous imprisonment without trial.[9]

The *Leinster Leader* also highlighted the plight of those un-sentenced prisoners from Kildare who were still being held without trial in Wakefield Detention Barracks. As no rebellion occurred in the county their continued detention, according to the paper, was 'to be deeply deplored'.[10] Eventually, in December, John Redmond made an impassioned plea to British Prime Minister David Lloyd George to release the prisoners as a Christmas gift to the Irish people. Bad publicity and the swing in public opinion forced the British to reconsider their Irish policy and on 21 December an amnesty was declared.[11] It was decided to release the internees from the north, south and west of Ireland first, followed by the men from Dublin and the midlands. This was to enable all the prisoners to be home for Christmas. A special train took 500 men to Holyhead and the first batch of 130 arrived in Kingstown (now Dun Laoghaire) on Saturday morning, 23 December. The return of the prisoners to Dublin was in marked contrast to their deportation seven months earlier. Huge crowds and bonfires greeted them. The men of 1916 returned as heroes to a people whose attitude had changed utterly since they had left.[12] Domhnall Ua Buachalla said, 'There was a noticeable change in the people now, and I received a royal welcome reception on reaching Maynooth.'[13]

One of those who had made good use of his time in Frongoch was Michael Smyth. He received a letter from Michael Collins in February 1917 telling him to get in touch with Patrick Colgan of Maynooth, with a view to reorganising the Volunteers in Kildare.

So, in early 1917 the Irish Volunteers were reorganised in Kildare by Smyth, Colgan and others and, at a meeting in Prosperous on Ascension Thursday, a battalion council was formed. It was decided to form it as the North Kildare Battalion. The following battalion officers were appointed: Patrick Colgan, Maynooth, commandant; Tom Harris, captain of the Prosperous Company, vice-commandant; Michael Smyth, Athgarvan, adjutant; and Art O'Connor, Celbridge, quartermaster. Officers from Maynooth, Celbridge, Prosperous, Carbury, Kill, Naas, Newbridge and Athgarvan were represented at the meeting.[14]

Two more companies were formed in Kildare town and Castle-dermot. In the south of the county Eamonn Malone, Barrowhouse, Athy, was appointed commandant of Carlow Brigade, which ex-tended into parts of Kildare, Wicklow and Laois. Éamon Ó Modhrain, Athgarvan, was appointed OC 6th Carlow Battalion, which had several companies from Kildare under its jurisdiction.[15] Michael Smyth recalled:

> An intensive organising campaign was carried out and a number of new Companies formed. I was employed on the training of the Companies in the Battalion area during 1917. I was also engaged at procuring arms and ammunition from British soldiers on the Curragh Camp.
>
> Eamonn [sic] Ó Modhrain and I went to the South Longford election in May 1917 when armed Volunteers were called for, and we were on duty in Longford town until polling day.[16]

The election candidate was Joseph McGuinness, a member of a prominent Longford family. At the time of the South Longford by-election he was in Lewes Jail for his part in the 1916 Rising.

Sinn Féin drafted republicans into Longford from all over the country to work on the campaign and McGuinness won by thirty-seven votes with the aid of one of the most effective election posters in Irish electoral history. It showed a man in prison uniform, with the slogan: 'Put him in to get him out'.[17]

On the night of 14 August 1917, in a surprise operation, RIC County Inspector Kerry Supple led a convoy of motor cars to different areas of the county, causing no little excitement when it was discovered that they were looking for weapons which had been held by the officers of the National Volunteers. These arms had been placed under the control of 'responsible' men in the different districts and the sudden midnight raid came as a surprise to all concerned. Rifles, swords and bayonets were seized at Newbridge, Ballymore and Rathangan and conveyed to the nearby constabulary barracks. The police quickly drove from district to district, finishing up about 6 a.m.[18]

In September 1917 forty republican prisoners, who had been rearrested in the months since the General Amnesty for Easter Rising prisoners in June 1917, began a hunger strike in Mountjoy Jail for political or prisoner-of-war status. Commandant Tom Ashe died in the Mater Hospital, Dublin, on 25 September, having been force fed. He had been arrested in Dublin in August and brought to Newbridge Barracks and then to the Curragh Camp where he was court-martialled. Michael Collins visited Ashe while he was held in the Curragh.[19] Kildare County Board GAA passed a resolution of sympathy to the relatives of Ashe, 'who died a victim for Ireland as a result of the callous and cruel treatment he was subjected to by the self-styled champions of Christianity and civilisation'.[20]

Ashe's funeral was organised by the IRB and was perhaps the greatest show of republican strength since the Rising. Thirty thousand people attended the funeral to Glasnevin Cemetery. Hundreds of Volunteers, representing all corners of the country, flanked the hearse. Michael Smyth said, 'The Companies of the North Kildare Battalion were mobilised for the Thomas Ashe funeral and formed cycling corps to Dublin for the funeral.'[21] After a volley of shots, Michael Collins stepped forward and announced: 'Nothing additional remains to be said. That volley which we just heard is the only speech which it is proper to make above the grave of a dead Fenian.'[22]

Sinn Féin poster advertising protest meeting at Naas, 1917.
Courtesy of Local Studies, Genealogy and Archives Dept,
Newbridge Library

At the Sinn Féin Convention in October 1917, Arthur Griffith graciously stepped down as president, to allow the election of de Valera, 'a soldier and a statesman', as president of the party Griffith had founded. De Valera brought unity to the party – disillusioned constitutional nationalists, members of the original Sinn Féin clubs, IRB and Volunteers were all brought together. It was agreed that a republic should be the desired objective of the party, but that a referendum would be held on the precise form of government once independence had been achieved. Nothing was said about the means by which British authority should be removed. Two days later, in an attempt to bring the political and military branches of the republican movement together, de Valera was also elected president of the Volunteers. Michael Collins became director of organisation and a number of IRB men were placed in key controlling positions on the Volunteer executive.[23] With the new leaders in place, the potential for re-organisation and co-ordination increased. Local initiative was encouraged. Michael Smyth recalled:

I mobilised the Athgarvan and Newbridge Companies for 1st November, 1917, when President de Valera's meeting was proclaimed in Newbridge.

I also had the Volunteers mobilised on the occasion of the public meeting addressed by the late Arthur Griffith, Joseph McGrath and other speakers in Naas in 1917. The meeting was proclaimed but was held outside the town.[24]

Throughout the latter half of 1917 Sinn Féin and the Irish Volunteers continued to gather support. Jim Dunne joined Kill Company in 1917 at the age of fifteen. His father, Patrick, had reorganised the company and acquired new arms, including revolvers, a .303 rifle, a new .38 Colt automatic and 1,200 rounds of ammunition. Jim and his brother Richard looked after the arms dump, which was a 'large tarred wooden box long enough to hold rifles and with its mouth opening in a well-covered ditch'. The youthful Volunteer was busy with dispatches, which consisted of 'long bicycle rides to Pitt's public house in Straffan, McLoughlin, tailor, Rathcoole, Co. Dublin, Monks, schoolmaster in Saggart, also to Newbridge and Two-Mile-House'.[25]

Patrick O'Carroll, Sallins Road, Naas, was employed with the *Leinster Leader* as a journalist. He joined Sinn Féin in 1917 and then progressed to active Volunteer status in the local IRA company:

When I joined the Naas Sinn Fein Club at its inception in 1917, I was one of those who had caught the contagion that sprung from the Rising a year before, the symptoms of which were a burning desire to justify the course taken by the men who had rebelled against the continuance of British rule in this country.[26]

The republican movement was in a good position when the British authorities began planning the extension of conscription to Ireland in the spring of 1918. In March 1918 the German army launched a huge offensive on the Western Front in a bid to end the Great War before the arrival of the new, fresh American army. Two British armies were flung back and thousands were killed, wounded or captured. Another huge offensive began on 9 April, again with enormous British losses. Britain looked towards Ireland to replace those lost. Conscription had been introduced in Britain in 1916, but John Dillon, the leader of the Irish Parliamentary Party after Redmond's death in March 1918, had insisted that only an Irish parliament could make such a serious decision for Ireland. The British government proposed to introduce compulsory military service in Ireland for all males between the ages of eighteen and fifty-one. Nationalists in Ireland united against conscription and Home Rulers and Sinn Féiners formed a committee to resist its implementation. Every county reported a considerable rise in Volunteer membership figures, and details were drawn up for resistance in the event of its implementation.[27]

Michael O'Kelly was at a well-attended anti-conscription protest outside Naas Town Hall on 15 April at which every different element of society was represented. D. J. Purcell, chairman of Naas UDC, presided, while other speakers were John O'Connor, MP; Rev. Fr Norris, Parish Priest (PP); M. Fitzsimons, UDC; and John Healy, Kildare County Council.[28] A statement from the Naas Board of Guardians demonstrated the kind of opposition:

> We, members of the Naas Board of Guardians, enter our most emphatic protest against the proposal to extend conscription to Ireland. We look upon the proposal as an exhibition of the worst form of Prussianism and a gross betrayal of the principles of liberty and rights of small nationalities, for which the Allied nations profess to be fighting. We consider that an attempt to conscript the manhood of Ireland without consultation with any Irish representatives can only result in plunging this country into turmoil and bloodshed.[29]

The conscription crisis finally brought both the church and moderate opinion into line with the Sinn Féin outlook. Despite

John Dillon's objections, the government pushed the Military Service Bill through the House of Commons on 16 April. In protest Dillon led the Irish Party out of the House of Commons and home to Ireland. Two days later a huge meeting was held in Dublin's Mansion House. Every strand of nationalist opinion was represented – de Valera and Griffith of Sinn Féin; Irish Party MPs John Dillon, Joe Devlin, William O'Brien and T. M. Healy; and W. O'Brien, president of the Irish Trades Union Congress. An anti-conscription pledge was drawn up to be signed at church doors the following Sunday.[30] It read:

> Denying the right of the British Government to enforce compulsory service in this country, we pledge ourselves solemnly to one another to resist conscription by the most effective means at our disposal.[31]

A delegation from the Mansion House conference conferred with archbishops and bishops then assembled at Maynooth College. The Catholic prelates meeting also issued a statement:

> We consider that conscription forced in this way upon Ireland is an oppressive and inhumane law which the Irish people have a right to resist by every means that are consonant with the law of God.[32]

On Sunday 21 April the pledge against conscription was signed by nearly the whole of nationalist Ireland, Catholics signing at the chapel door. Protest meetings against conscription were held throughout the country. Anti-conscription meetings were held throughout Kildare, some of them the largest gatherings seen since the days of the Land League.[33]

At a huge meeting in Newbridge, on the proposition of P. J. Doyle, chairman, Naas Board of Guardians, and seconded by Jack Fitzgerald, chairman, Kildare County Board GAA, the following resolution was adopted, amidst a scene of much enthusiasm:

> That all political parties into which the lovers of Ireland are at present unhappily divided, should now come together and join in expressing an undivided opinion on the supremely important question of conscription in Ireland. That we are prepared to support by every means in our power the principle laid down by the Catholic Bishops, priests and people of Ireland, that compulsory service in Ireland can and ought to be made operative only with the free consent of the Irish people given in a clear and constitutional way. That such consent has been neither given nor asked for, and that in the existing circumstances the conscription of Irishmen is an act of tyranny, certain to be followed by consequences of disaster to public and private order, safety and peace. That having made this, our protest, we declare our determination in the circumstances to stand loyally together in all lawful and effective forms of resistance that shall be devised for us by our leaders in Ireland.[34]

Michael O'Kelly was present at a large demonstration in Naas on 23 April, when the assembly:

> … registered a pledge to defeat conscription, in token of which all present held up the right hand while the pledge was being read from the platform. An Anti-Conscription Committee was

then formed of which N. P. Byrne and Seumas O'Kelly were appointed Joint Honorary Secretaries.[35]

While some were prepared to use peaceful means, others were preparing for all-out war to resist conscription. The Volunteers began raiding police barracks for arms and the Labour Party called a one-day general strike. The whole country, with the exception of Belfast, closed down on 25 April.[36]

A major crackdown on Sinn Féin began and on 17–18 May over 100 Sinn Féin and Volunteer leaders were arrested in the name of the 'German Plot', charged with plotting with Germany to foment another rebellion in Ireland. The pretext for this was the landing of Joseph Dowling, a member of Roger Casement's ill-fated Irish Brigade, on the Galway coast from a German U-boat. However, Michael Collins had a spy in Dublin Castle, Kildareman Ned Broy, who was attached to G Division – the intelligence division of the Dublin Metropolitan Police (DMP). He had supplied Collins with a list of prominent republicans due to be arrested and some, like Collins, avoided capture.

On 2 July a proclamation banned Sinn Féin, the Irish Volunteers, Cumann na mBan, the Gaelic League and the GAA, all of them proclaimed as 'dangerous organisations'. In defiance of this the GAA organised matches and games throughout the country. Gaelic Sunday, 9 August, became a day of massive national defiance of the Defence of the Realm Act. Seventeen matches were fixed for Kildare. Martial law was declared in large areas of the country.

As republican activity increased, so too did police arrests and harassment. In August, three men – J. J. Byrne, Mick Sammon and

T. Stapleton – were arrested after reading the Sinn Féin manifesto outside churches in Athy, Kilcullen and Kilcock. All were taken to Naas RIC Barracks. The police who escorted Stapleton from Kilcock had considerable difficulty in getting a car in Naas to convey them back again to their station. The three republicans were sentenced to six months' imprisonment. Police later tore down posters announcing a Sinn Féin meeting at Hodgestown, near Donadea.[37] In Naas, Tommy Patterson and Jimmy Whyte were charged with obstructing police who attempted to enter the Town Hall where Laurence Ginnell, MP, and Fr Thomas Burbage were speaking at an anti-conscription meeting. Ginnell was sentenced to six months', Patterson received three months' and Whyte two months' imprisonment.[38]

During a proclaimed meeting in Naas in the late summer, which demanded the release of the political prisoners, the RIC turned out in strength to arrest Art O'Connor, who was to speak. O'Connor was a much-wanted man at the time. Born on 18 May 1888 at Elm Hall, Loughlinstown, Celbridge, he was educated at Holy Faith School, Celbridge, and Blackrock College, Dublin (where he met Éamon de Valera). He then attended Trinity College, Dublin, for which he needed special permission because he was a Catholic. He graduated in 1911 with an engineering degree and was immediately employed by Kildare County Council. His elder brother, James, later became a judge in the republican courts, while his younger brother, Seán (Jack), a former pupil of St Enda's, was also active and was later interned in the Curragh. Two of his sisters, Francis and Brigid, were active in Cumann na mBan. O'Connor, an enthusiastic supporter of the GAA and an active member of the Gaelic League, joined Sinn Féin in 1914. The following year he was among a small number of individuals elected onto the organising committee of the Irish Volunteers in north Kildare.[39]

Volunteers from Naas, Newbridge and Kill Companies surrounded the platform while O'Connor addressed the meeting. The police made no attempt to interfere until he stepped down from the platform. The Volunteers linked hands and formed two double lines from the platform to a laneway where O'Connor was to make good his escape. The police charged the gathering with batons, but Volunteers held a flagstaff to bar their passage to the lane, while O'Connor was safely spirited away. A bicycle was waiting for him and two cyclists, John and Peadar Traynor of Woolpack, Kill, escorted him to a safe house at Arthurstown, Kill. O'Connor was later arrested in Spiddal, County Galway, and imprisoned in Durham Jail in connection with the so-called 'German Plot' (an alleged treasonable plot between Sinn Féin and Germany that was used as an excuse to intern suspected dissidents).[40]

That evening, as the members of Kill Company were leaving Naas, they were attacked by about thirty British soldiers, many of them locals home on furlough. Their wives and girlfriends joined in the fray 'assisting with bottles'. According to Jim Dunne:

> They had hoisted a Union Jack on a telegraph pole. Our men charged them, took down the flag and put them to flight. Captain P. Dunne received a stab wound from a knife, in the hand, and Lieutenant T. Domican received head injuries when struck by a bottle.[41]

Recruits flocked in their thousands to the Volunteers, pledging to fight all attempts by Britain to introduce conscription. By autumn the Volunteers had 100,000 members. Eventually, the British authorities were dissuaded from introducing conscription simply because they realised that it would require more troops to police conscription than its enforcement would produce.[42]

The Volunteers now attempted to rearm themselves. Most of their arms had been surrendered during the Rising. Local units began to collect shotguns from supporters or steal them if necessary. These were some of the first offensive actions taken by many units. One of the first raids for arms in County Kildare was in the Athy area. On the night of 10 October 1918 a party of armed men visited the homes of farmers on the Queen's County (Laois) and Kildare sides of Athy looking for arms. One man, Henry Hosie, resisted demands to stand aside and surrender. In a scuffle he received a blow to the head with an unidentified weapon. It was stated that he had thrown a lamp at the raiders, who left without securing any firearms. In other districts some weapons were taken, with no opposition offered and no violence used. This was the first raid for arms in the district, which was noted as being a recruitment area for the British Army. The raids were widely condemned and the general opinion was that the raiders were from outside the area as they had travelled there on bicycles.[43]

The Great War ended on 11 November 1918 and with it went the threat of conscription. Armistice Day was a day of great celebration throughout the British Empire. In Naas the Union Jack was hoisted over the courthouse and *The Kildare Observer* reported on 16 November that:

... there was a general feeling of relief, if there was little outward manifestation of jubilation. Towards evening there was some flag waving by the military, who later indulged in pranks and demonstrations to show their joy at the termination of the war.

Some of the shops and houses in the town and its vicinity also displayed the British flag. In Newbridge and the Curragh, the *Observer* reported that the military celebrated 'with flag waving, cheering and other demonstrations of joy'. The Newbridge Town Commission passed a resolution of congratulations to the Allies on their victory. The town of Celbridge was brilliantly illuminated for the victory celebrations, the revelry continuing in the streets until the small hours of the morning, and there were celebrations in every town and village.[44]

Some 30,000 Irishmen died in what was known as the 'War to end all wars'. After the Armistice more than 100,000 veterans returned as civilians to Ireland.[45]

A general election followed the end of the war. A Sinn Féin candidate was put forward for every constituency in the country with the exception of Trinity College, Dublin. As a demonstration of unity Labour withdrew from the election to keep the nationalist vote solid. Whereas the Irish Party campaigned on a promise of a return to Westminster and a renewal of their fight for Home Rule, Sinn Féin promised to abstain from the British parliament, form a government in Dublin and look for the recognition of the Irish Republic, proclaimed in 1916, at the Paris Peace Conference. The Irish electoral register was revised and women over thirty were given the franchise to vote for the first time, increasing the electorate one-and-a-half times. The Sinn Féin candidates in County Kildare were Domhnall Ua Buachalla (Maynooth) for

North Kildare and Art O'Connor (Celbridge) for South Kildare. The Irish Party nominees were the sitting members of both constituencies – John O'Connor in North Kildare and Denis Kilbride in South Kildare.[46]

Some days prior to polling day, on 2 December, Fr Michael O'Flanagan and Dr Grogan of Maynooth arrived with Domhnall Ua Buachalla in Naas to address a meeting at the Market Square Weigh House in support of the Sinn Féin candidates. Fr O'Flanagan was known as an eloquent speaker and there was a large receptive crowd in the square, but as the patriotic priest concluded his address, a mob of British soldiers and women congregated at the outskirts of the crowd and began to indulge in cries of 'Up the red, white and blue', and 'Up England'. Ua Buachalla then mounted the podium. The hecklers quietened down, but in the course of his speech Ua Buachalla pointed to a small Union Jack the soldiers had hoisted on a lamp-post outside the post office and said this was the flag under which Ireland was forced to live, but it would be soon replaced by the flag of Sinn Féin. Some youths left the crowd and walked circuitously towards the post office. When within a few yards of the lamp-post they made a dash for it and one of them was pushed up towards the Union Jack. He managed to get hold of the flag before he was spotted by the soldiers who rushed after him. The youths ran with their prize into the crowd. The soldiers pursued them and fists flew as tempers sparked. As the police pulled the soldiers back, some of the Sinn Féin stewards got between the hotheads and order was restored. Cheers and counter-cheers were then indulged in while the soldiers hoisted another Union Jack on the lamp-post. The situation calmed down and the meeting was brought to a close.[47]

As the motorcars conveying the Sinn Féin candidate and his supporters drove away from the meeting, there was cheering from some and booing from others. One car drew up outside the Royal Hotel, and a few minutes later some girls advanced to it and pulled off a Sinn Féin flag attached to it. They only managed to carry their trophy a few yards when it was taken back by the young man in charge of the car and put back in position. The girls fled down a laneway. By this time the crowd had dispersed.[48]

Not all ex-servicemen were enemies of Sinn Féin. Thomas Curran (Naas) joined the British Army in 1914 and served with the Royal Dublin Fusiliers. He was discharged on health grounds in 1916 and joined Sinn Féin on his return to Naas. Curran became one of the organisers of the 1918 elections in County Kildare.

At the conclusion of polling on the day of the election, the ballot boxes were conveyed to the County Courthouse at Naas. The ballot boxes at the Town Hall polling station were taken possession of by the presiding officers, who were ex-RIC men, and were escorted by a party of local Volunteers, under the charge of Alfie Sweeney, to the courthouse, where a guard was posted outside the room in which the boxes were deposited. The Volunteers guarded them overnight, until they were taken possession of the following morning by the returning officer, when the counting of votes commenced. Patrick O'Keefe (Kilcock), who joined the Irish Volunteers in 1914, recalled escorting ballot boxes from Kilcock to Naas during the general election of 1918.[49]

Despite heavy rain, a large crowd assembled outside the courthouse in Naas to hear the results announced on the evening of 28 December. Domhnall Ua Buachalla was elected MP for North Kildare, while Art O'Connor was elected for South Kildare. The results in North Kildare were: Domhnall Ua Buachalla (SF) 5,979; John O'Connor (IP) 2,772. With 13,000 people on the register and 8,855 votes recorded, Ua Buachalla had a clear majority of 3,207, the largest majority ever in North Kildare. In South Kildare, Art O'Connor (SF) was elected with 7,104 votes, while Denis Kilbride (IP) received 1,545, giving O'Connor a majority of 5,559. The election was an overwhelming victory for the republicans. Sinn Féin won seventy-three of 105 seats throughout the country – forty-seven of the candidates were in jail. The unionists won twenty-six seats, a gain of eight on their previous showing, but the biggest losers were the Irish Party, who were practically routed. They won only six seats, compared with their pre-election sixty-eight seats. Of the thirty-two counties, twenty-four had returned only republican members.[50]

There was great cheering when Domhnall Ua Buachalla's return was announced. On leaving the building the successful candidate was again loudly cheered. During the day the count was carried out in the best of humour and the only unseemly incident was when Tom Domican was struck on the head by a stone thrown by a woman while the crowd was being addressed by Ua Buachalla and other Sinn Féin dignitaries from the windows of the Royal Hotel, Main Street, Naas, after the declaration of the result. After nightfall most of the houses in Naas were illuminated and a torchlight procession was formed and marched through the streets headed by a fife and drum band. Later a public meeting was held in the Market Square and addressed by D. Murphy, vice-president of the local Sinn Féin branch, and other local speakers. There was also a torchlight procession in Newbridge when the results were received.

The announcement of the results from the Town Hall, Athy, was received with a great outburst of cheering by a large crowd of local supporters who marched through the town shouting 'Up O'Connor' and singing republican songs. Art O'Connor was still in an English prison, but he was ably represented by a Mr Keating. The town was decorated with republican colours during the day and, as at Naas, there were no untoward incidents. Athy was a strong unionist town and the result was a surprise, with Sinn Féin even picking up votes in the Curragh Camp.

Great jubilation was also displayed in Monasterevin on receipt of the election results. The local fife and drum band led a march through the town. A large bonfire was lit near the canal harbour and most houses were illuminated. On the next night a bonfire was lit at Lughill and a large contingent from Monasterevin, accompanied by the band, marched in a torchlight procession to Kildangan, where another bonfire was lit.[51]

The Irish Times of 30 December 1918 announced:

Sinn Féin has swept the board, but we do not know – does itself know? – what it intends to do with its victory. The defeat of the Nationalist Party is crushing and final … Ireland has elected 73 Sinn Féin members, and none of them for the present, at any rate, will attend the Imperial Parliament. In other words, the country outside North-East Ulster … is virtually disenfranchised. It is an impossible situation as Sinn Féin will soon discover …

The electoral victory for Sinn Féin was overwhelming. In Kildare it seemed that the electorate had accepted the mood that was sweeping the country.

4

WAR COMES TO KILDARE

The general election was not the only indication of sweeping change in Kildare. Sinn Féin leaders in the county encouraged agrarian agitation, including cattle driving and the levelling of stone fencing on the lands of large graziers. They saw the opportunity to exploit the land question and win support by associating themselves with the agitation. For the first time in years County Kildare was mentioned in the county inspectors' monthly reports as being in 'an unsatisfactory condition'. Disturbances were linked to agrarianism. In January 1918 there had been eleven cattle drives around Kill in opposition to the eleven-month lease-holding system, and some of Lord Mayo's grazing tenants' cattle were driven off the land. (Lord Mayo of Palmerstown was a leading unionist and a major landowner in the area.) Twenty extra policemen were drafted into Kill to prevent cattle driving in the area and were housed in the local village hall. In February the number of cattle drives rose to twenty-three and County Inspector Supple ascribed 'the great majority to Sinn Fein influence'. Labourers and small farmers were reported to be joining Sinn Féin in large numbers. The conscription crisis and the May arrests, allied to the land agitation, increased support for Sinn Féin and by July there were twenty-five Sinn Féin clubs in the county, with 1,814 members.[1]

On 1 January 1919 a pantomime was held in the village hall in Kill in aid of the fund for payment of the district nurse. The concert ended about 10 p.m. and a number of lamps that had been used in the hall were carefully extinguished. About 2 a.m. the RIC was notified that the hall was blazing: the police barracked in the hall had been lured away by reports of cattle driving, while Volunteers, taking advantage of their absence, burned it. The hall had been built in 1914 and paid for by public subscriptions and donations by Lord and Lady Mayo of Palmerstown Demesne. The wooden structure cost £220 to build and could accommodate 240 people. In August 1917 the secretary of the Sinn Féin club of Ardclough and Kill had written to Lady Mayo demanding the hall for the purpose of meetings, on the grounds that as the hall had been built by public subscriptions they were entitled to use it. The letter was signed by Thomas Clarke, New Row, Kill. To that letter Lady Mayo replied stating that the use of the hall could not be given, as under its rules it could only be used for educational or recreational purposes. According to Lord and Lady Mayo the RIC were billeted in the hall without their permission. The hall and its contents, which included 150 chairs and a piano, were totally destroyed.[2]

On 21 January 1919 the newly elected Sinn Féin members of the British House of Commons who were at liberty met in the Mansion House, Dublin, and instituted the first Dáil Éireann, or Irish Assembly. They had refused to go to Westminster, setting up a parliament of their own. Those MPs present called themselves

Teachtaí Dála (TDs), representatives of the Dáil. At the first
Dáil sitting, Robert Barton, representing Kildare/Wicklow, read
the English version of the 'Message to the Free Nations of the
World', which asked nations to recognise Ireland as a separate
nation, free from British rule. Domhnall Ua Buachalla was also
present, representing Kildare. The Irish elected representatives,
having already approved a provisional constitution, confirmed
the Proclamation that Patrick Pearse had read on the steps of the
GPO in 1916, and ratified the establishment of the Irish Republic. They pledged Dáil Éireann and the people 'to make this declaration effective by every means at our command' and demanded
'the evacuation of our country by the British Garrison'.[3]

On the same day, in what *The Kildare Observer* described as 'a
revolting murder', two RIC men were shot dead at Soloheadbeg,
County Tipperary, by Volunteers firing the first shots of what
became known as the War of Independence, or the Anglo-Irish
War.[4] This 'war' was one of opportunity, rather than an action of
meticulous planning. It happened rather because of the ineptitude
of British policy, graphically illustrated by the government's
ignoring of the results of the 1918 general election. Hardline
republicans, such as Dan Breen and Seán Treacy in Tipperary, fed
up with the slow progress of events, acted on their own initiative
to try to start a war, and they succeeded.

In County Kildare the first episode of the War of Independence occurred on 13 February at the Curragh, when a local farmer
was shot dead by a British sentry, Private Gay. Patrick Gavin was
driving a cow to Newbridge fair at 5 a.m., when Gay challenged
him as he passed the Tully pumping station. Gavin failed to halt
and the soldier fired one shot hitting Gavin in the chest, mortally

wounding him. At the hearing at which Private Gay was charged with the killing, the sergeant of the guard, Duke of Wellington's Regiment, gave evidence that he heard Gay call out and then the sound of a rifle shot. Private Gay claimed that Gavin had attacked him with a stick and that he was in fear for his life. Gay also claimed that he thought more men could have been hiding in nearby hedges. Two other soldiers, who were part of the guard, produced a stick, but Gavin's employer, Joseph Moore, said it was not like any other that Patrick usually had with him. He also said that the cow was in calf, so he would not have allowed Patrick Gavin to carry a stick like the one produced. On completion of the evidence the coroner pointed out to the jury the most important point of the evidence produced and after a very long consideration the verdict was delivered, which was reported in the *Leinster Leader* on 15 February:

> That Patrick Gavin died of haemorrhage caused by a bullet which severed the main artery of the heart, fired by Private Gay and all of us are of opinion that Private Gay did not exercise sufficient discretion on this occasion and that before firing he should have consulted an older head in the person of the sergeant of the guard and we are of opinion that for the safety of the public in such places more experienced men should be placed on sentry duty. Some light should be shown at night time as a warning to the public of the presence of a military guard. Considering the circumstances of Patrick Gavin's death we will draw the attention of the military authorities to the relatives of the deceased.

When the remains were removed there was a very large gathering of sympathisers from the town and district where Patrick Gavin was well known. The inquest reported: 'He is spoken of as a decent man who was very popular in the neighbourhood and much regret is expressed by his employer and the people of the neighbourhood at his untimely death'. Patrick Gavin (45) was an unmarried man who had worked for Joseph Moore for fifteen years. It was thought that he had a hearing problem and did not hear the sentry's challenge. Private Gay was discharged from the court.[5]

In the same month Michael Collins and Harry Boland engineered the escape of Éamon de Valera from Lincoln Jail. De Valera took refuge in the home of Dr Robert P. Farnan at 5 Merrion Square, Dublin. Born in Moone, County Kildare, Dr Farnan was at one time president of the Land League in Kildare. Regular Sinn Féin and Irish Volunteer meetings were held at his home in Dublin, which later became de Valera's headquarters. A trusted friend, he accompanied de Valera to London to meet the British Prime Minister, Lloyd George, in July 1921, and also brokered talks between de Valera and Richard Mulcahy to try to avoid civil war in 1922.[6]

On 6 March Pierce McCan, a newly elected member of Dáil Éireann for East Tipperary, died from the flu epidemic in Gloucester Prison. The escape of de Valera and the death of McCan forced the British to decide upon a general release of the 'German Plot' prisoners in Britain. A torchlight procession led by a local band welcomed Kildare TD Art O'Connor home to Celbridge after his release from Durham Jail. O'Connor was home in time to attend the second session of the Dáil held between 1 and 4 April. This and subsequent meetings were held in various places and in private, and were chiefly concerned with plans for the future development of the Irish economy, if and when Dáil Éireann became free to function normally.[7] The Dáil had taken over as far as possible all functions of government, but was not allowed to continue peacefully due to harassment and arrests by the British.

Having resumed his work with Kildare County Council as an engineer, O'Connor applied for and was granted permission to work for the Dáil wherever he was sent throughout the country. He was appointed director of agriculture when Robert Barton was arrested in January 1920, and took a particular interest in the setting up of the Land Arbitration Courts.[8] These courts dealt with age-old land disputes and were so successful that landlords who were being harassed for possession of their lands appealed to them and not the British authorities.

At a meeting on 10 April, the Dáil called for a boycott of the RIC. This idea, rather than outright attacks, appealed to those in the movement such as de Valera and Arthur Griffith, who were wary of escalating violence. The Soloheadbeg killings had caused great distress and had not been authorised by the republican leadership. Many in Sinn Féin felt that ordinary nationalists would not tolerate a campaign of killing policemen.

The RIC was mainly Catholic – in 1914 the religious breakdown of the force had been 81 per cent Catholic and 19 per cent Protestant. Most of the recruits came from farming stock, usually younger sons who would not inherit the family farm. Recruits were not allowed to serve in the county of their birth and if they married were not permitted to serve in the county of their wife's birth. The RIC was a civilian force, but was organised and trained much like the military police, although up to 1916 it rarely carried firearms. By 1919 the role of the RIC had changed completely as the political situation deteriorated. Now the RIC was busy conducting searches for arms and wanted persons. In the years of land agitation and civil unrest, the RIC had been to the forefront of implementing the law. It had since become the focus of the distrust and hatred of the affected people, so it was the police rather than the military who became the main targets of the Volunteers.

In many respects the boycott resembled an economic blockade and had a tremendous impact from 1919 onward. Merchants refused to serve the police, the men and their families were shunned and threatened, and people who violated the boycott risked punishment themselves. Recruits were intimidated and police property, such as bicycles, was stolen.[9]

Meanwhile, the republican movement was building an alternative state. Agitation between the Transport Workers' Union and the County Kildare Farmers' Union led to strikes, picketing and violent incidents in the county, in which republicans were heavily involved. The Transport Workers' Union had made representation to the Farmers' Union in respect of pay rises from the minimum wage of 30s per week to 45s for agricultural labourers. On 11 April the Farmers' Union stated that it could not accept the principle of raising the minimum wage beyond what was fixed by the Irish Agricultural Wages Board, on which the workers were fully represented. The Transport Workers' Union asked for the opening of negotiations with the Farmers' Union, which referred back to its statement of 11 April.[10] Republicans were involved in a strike by agricultural labourers employed by Edward Kennedy on his estate at Bishopscourt, Kill. The men who remained in Kennedy's employment were supplied with food from the nearby Dew Drop Inn, which led to the Transport Workers' Union picketing the premises. Some time later four picketers were charged with assaulting Henry Stratford, an employee of Kennedy, and taking a loaded revolver from him near the Bishopscourt estate. The four members of the Kill branch of the Transport Workers' Union charged were Peter Mulhall, Thomas Farrell, William Carroll and Christopher Mills. Farrell was bound to the peace from the start of the Bishopscourt dispute, while Mulhall also had a case pending. Mills was a member of Kill Company, Irish Volunteers, and Pat Dunne, OC Kill Company, posted the four men's bail bond.[11]

Continuing efforts were made to introduce trade unionism amongst farm labourers. At Lewistown, near Naas, a large rick of hay was burned in mid-April, while the following month flax and machinery belonging to a Belfast firm was destroyed by fire at Cooltrim, Donadea.[12]

In June 1919 Éamon de Valera went to America, determined to win political recognition for the Irish Republic he represented and to collect funds for the Irish war. Britain had no one to counter de Valera's triumphant campaign and $8 million flowed into the coffers of the Irish National Loan. (In Ireland Michael Collins, as Minister of Finance, floated the loan.) De Valera clashed with the old Fenian John Devoy, who was unwilling to relinquish control of Irish-American affairs. Devoy, then seventy-seven, was the last active Fenian. His hearing was nearly gone and he was troubled with cataracts. He was suspicious of his allies in Clan na Gael and, although he was fond of de Valera, the two could not get along. The conflict that soon erupted has often been portrayed as a clash of personalities, de Valera versus Devoy. De

Valera believed that the American organisations existed to serve the Irish Republic and as its representative he wanted to control them. Devoy, of course, was not about to hand over the reins of the organisation he had rebuilt from the ashes of disarray. In the end de Valera formed his own organisation, the American Association for the Recognition of the Irish Republic. Contact between Clan na Gael and the IRB was terminated and the Irish-American movement, to which John Devoy had devoted his life, was split down the middle. De Valera did not return to Ireland until Christmas 1920, his quest for American government recognition of the Irish Republic having failed.[13]

On 24 June 1919 Roman Catholic bishops, assembled in Maynooth, condemned British rule in Ireland, describing it as 'the rule of the sword, utterly unsuited to a civilised nation and extremely provocative of disorder and chronic rebellion'.[14]

In Athy, a huge crowd gathered on Saturday 12 July to welcome home demobilised British soldiers. However, republican prisoners were also being released and one from Athy was due to return on the same day. The Union Jack was hoisted over the Town Hall in honour of the soldiers. Both groups met and, with cries of 'Up the rebels' and 'Up the khaki', set into each other with boots and fists, although no serious injuries were inflicted. On the following day the County Kildare Feis, which was held in the town, was disrupted when around fifty ex-servicemen attacked and gutted the house formerly used by the local Sinn Féin club. Police reinforcements had to be called in to quell the disturbances.[15]

At the beginning of July a campaign of strike action began in Celbridge when sixty labourers, all members of the County Kildare Farmers' Union, were taken out on strike because their employers refused to deviate from their union's decision not to negotiate with the Transport Workers' Union over wages and working hours. The Farmers' Union then informed the Transport Workers' Union that, unless the Celbridge men resumed work, there would be a general lockout of all members of the Transport Workers' Union employed by members of the Farmers' Union. In the face of this threat the Transport Workers' Union co-ordinated a strike throughout the county that soon spread to County Meath.[16] Offending farms were blockaded and strikers wielding clubs prevented the movement of goods, disrupted fairs and auctions, engaged in cattle drives and damaged crops.

From an agricultural standpoint the strike was disastrous. Crops suffered severely – especially the hay crop – and about 1,000 men were idle. Shops in towns and villages which supplied farmers and their families identified with the Farmers' Union were picketed. Markets were abandoned as no produce was allowed to be sold; haycocks were scattered; oat crops trampled; cattle and horses driven into planted fields. In early August extra police were drafted into the county, which led to a considerable relaxation of 'picketing and interference with farmers'.[17]

Republicans were quite active in the strike, as Michael Smyth recalled:

I had to arrange for protection with Volunteers in each area dur-ing the big Farm Strike of 1919 in North Kildare in which the Volunteers were kept busy doing police duty for about four months.[18]

Patrick Colgan maintained that the farmers approached the RIC for armed protection:

I approached the farmers' leaders and told them unless they refused R.I.C. protection I would encourage the strikers to attack those protected and the R.I.C. as well. I offered to see that order was kept. It was a ticklish assignment as many of the strikers were Volunteers. We managed to keep both sides within bounds.[19]

A settlement was negotiated between the Athy branch of the Farmers' Union and the Transport Workers' Union on 20 August, which agreed a wage increase to 32*s* per week of six working days of ten hours for men over twenty and 26*s* for men between eighteen and twenty, from the date of resumption of work. The strike in the rest of the county continued until a further agreement was reached on 23 August 1919.[20]

Political disturbances in the county continued: in August a railway signal cabin at Caragh, near Naas, was torched; thousands of bales of hay were burned at Newbridge Military Barracks the following month; and five masked and armed men raided the Naas Gas Works and cut off the gas supply to the town.[21]

As the Dáil began to function effectively, the Volunteer organisation recognised it as the legal government of Ireland and came directly under the control of the Minister for Defence, Cathal Brugha. He took full responsibility for the military actions of the Volunteers, who from that time became known as the Irish Republican Army (IRA). Each officer and volunteer took an Oath of Allegiance to the Government of the Irish Republic. The Minister for Home Affairs, Austin Stack, proceeded to set up a system of arbitration courts and a republican police force was also founded, drawn from local IRA companies. By the end of 1919 the 700-year-old British legal system had broken down to such an extent that even those opposed to Sinn Féin were taking their civil actions to republican courts. In Dublin, Michael Collins orchestrated violent attacks on members of the intelligence-gathering G Division, including the killing of Detective Patrick 'Dog' Smyth, on 20 July 1919, whose wife was a native of Waterstown, Sallins, and who was holidaying there when her husband was shot. On 10 September 1919 Dublin Castle reacted by banning Dáil Éireann, Sinn Féin, the Volunteers and Cumann na mBan.[22]

In November 1919 the Irish Committee of the British government, which had been set up in April 1918 to draw up a Home Rule Bill for Ireland, issued a report to the British cabinet (with an accompanying request for special secrecy), which stated:

> ... in view of the situation in Ireland itself, of public opinion in the Dominions, and in the United States of America, they cannot recommend the policy of either repealing or of postponing the Home Rule Act of 1914. In their judgement it is essential, now that the war is over, and the peace Conference has dealt with so many analogous questions in Europe, that the Government should make a sincere attempt to deal with the Irish question once and for all.[23]

The committee foresaw two stumbling blocks – the break-up of the Empire by the establishment of an Irish Republic and the placing of Ulster under the rule of an Irish parliament. The committee recommended to the cabinet that two parliaments should be set up in Ireland, linked by a Council of Ireland, with reserved powers. This type of Home Rule, which was agreeable to Britain, was far short of what Sinn Féin was asking for. In the coming months the republican response became clear.

On the night of 3 January 1920 five Volunteers from Naas Company attacked the home of County Inspector Kerry Supple on the Sallins Road, which was halfway between Naas and the village of Sallins. Jimmy Whyte, Peter Gill, Gus Fitzpatrick, Tom Patterson and Mick Byrne fired a fusillade of revolver shots at Supple's house, which was under guard by RIC men from Naas Barracks. The bullets hit a lower window that faced the road. A couple of large windowpanes were broken and some furniture received bullet marks. Supple, his wife and servants occupied the house at the time, though none were injured. Armed police patrols were stepped up in the area after the attack.[24]

Notwithstanding the landslide victory for Sinn Féin at the general election, opponents of the republicans had contended that the majority obtained by Sinn Féin was due largely to the threat of conscription. They further argued that Sinn Féin had no mandate for establishing Dáil Éireann and that the Irish people did not approve of the IRA's war against the crown forces. In the municipal and urban elections, which were held throughout the country on 15 January 1920, this assertion was put to the test. The councils – which administered affairs in Irish towns and cities, levying rates and controlling certain local services – were directly responsible to the Local Government Board of the Dublin Castle administration, which kept the machinery of local government firmly under its control. The British government had introduced a new system of voting, known as proportional representation, with the intention of giving increased representation to the unionist minority of the population in an attempt to reduce the Sinn Féin majority at the polls. The fact that Sinn Féin approved the introduction of proportional representation surprised many observers. The government assumed that the mass of the Irish people, which formed the chief support for Sinn Féin, were uneducated and would be confused by the new and intricate system and would spoil their votes. However, instruction in the new system was carried out by the Sinn Féin organisation with such thoroughness that the number of spoiled votes recorded was less than 2.5 per cent.[25]

Despite the handicaps of arrests and harassment, the result of the election was an overwhelming vote of confidence in the republican government and a clear indication of popular support for self-determination. Sinn Féin, though banned, in close co-operation with Labour – who were strong supporters of the republican ideal – won control of eleven out of twelve cities and boroughs in Ireland. The only municipal council left under unionist control was Belfast. Out of 206 councils elected throughout the country, 172 were returned with a republican majority – Sinn Féin won 550 seats. From these councils came formal resolutions pledging allegiance to the Irish Republic and to Dáil Éireann. All relations with the British-run Local Government Board were broken off. Henceforth the republican government was the sole authority acknowledged by these municipal and urban councils. Dublin Castle abandoned all aid to these new authorities, causing them enormous problems in providing the necessary staff to oversee a new system and in collecting rates and revenues. However, the new councils accepted their responsibilities and found ways to cope.[26]

Levels of IRA activity throughout the country differed greatly from area to area. The biggest disincentive to republican activity in Kildare was undoubtedly the large military presence in the county. The presence of the military had been of great economic advantage to the county, and the town of Newbridge had practically sprung up around the army barracks.[27] However, it made carrying out any action there very difficult for the IRA during the War of Independence. In 1920 there were three infantry battalions, two cavalry regiments and supporting divisional troops amounting to 4,300 soldiers in the Curragh. There were a further 800 soldiers in Kildare town's artillery barracks, 673 in Newbridge and 130 in Naas. At the beginning of April 1920 a training depot was also opened at the Curragh for English recruits to the RIC. This made Kildare one of the most militarised counties in the country.

One unforeseen benefit of this presence was that disgruntled, and entrepreneurial, soldiers were a boon to the IRA. On 29 April 1920 men from L Battery, Royal Horse Artillery, sold local IRA members seventeen revolvers, along with 723 rounds of ammunition.[28]

The arms depot at the Curragh should have been an obvious target for IRA men looking to raid for guns and ammunition, although it was considered to be 'well protected and not liable to attack by the rebels' and remained the main issuing depot for the Gun and Machine Gun sections of the army and the police. There were also, by the end of 1919, 10,000 seized and surrendered arms, as well as explosives and ammunition in the Ordnance Depot Stores.[29]

However, it was not the British Army, but the RIC that was the main target of the IRA, and in 1920 new forces emerged on the scene to institute a more ruthless campaign against that organisation.

5

A DEPLORABLE STATE

In the months following the success of Sinn Féin at the polls in January 1920, there was a marked intensification of crown forces' activity, including the killing of several Sinn Féin elected representatives by elements of the RIC. Republican activity was also on the increase and the campaign of gun attacks and intimidation on the RIC and DMP was beginning to have a telling effect on the morale of the police. A substantial number of policemen began to resign from the RIC for safety reasons and because of a conflict of loyalty. To counter the fall-off, the authorities started to recruit for the RIC in England as well as Ireland. Recruiting offices were opened in London, Liverpool and Manchester in December 1919 and by 15 April 1920 some 400 men had been enlisted. Unemployment was high in Britain and service in the RIC was seen as an opportunity for excitement and adventure for which recruits would receive £3 10s per week, a uniform and cost-of-living expenses. Nearly 90 per cent of the recruits were English, with 10 per cent from Scotland and Wales. A few came from the Dominions. The majority, almost 90 per cent, were ex-servicemen.

The standard training course for the new British recruits was of six weeks' duration as compared with six months for ordinary RIC recruits. As they were nearly all ex-soldiers they needed no training in musketry, firearms instruction or drill. They received only rudimentary training in police duties and were then assigned to RIC barracks in the most troublesome areas of the country. The large influx of recruits left the RIC with a shortage of police uniforms, so army khaki had to be issued as well, leaving the new recruits with a mixture of bottle-green and khaki. When they appeared on the streets of Limerick in their motley uniforms they became known as the 'Black and Tans', named after a local pack of hounds. The name would soon come to inspire hatred and terror, and they gained an infamous place in Irish history.[1]

Michael O'Kelly wrote of these men, rather incorrectly:

The resignations of members of the [RIC] Force, some of them from motives of repugnance to the work expected of them, next set in, and to fill the gaps in the ranks and convert the Force into a marauding murder organisation more in keeping with British traditions of waging war against the Irish, the jails, workhouses and slums of England were raked for recruits to serve the R.I.C. So came the Black and Tans to take the offensive against the I.R.A., supported by the huge regular army of occupation.[2]

What is not in doubt is that the arrival of the Black and Tans escalated the violence throughout the country.

A section of Black and Tans was based in No. 2 barrack at the military depot in Naas, which was fenced off from the soldiers' area; a barbed wire fence halved the barrack square and the Black and Tans occupied one section. A section of the new recruits was also based in a large three-storey building in Kildare town, known as the Clubhouse, for a time.[3]

On 30 March 1920, five days after the arrival of the first English recruits, the IRA issued a proclamation, which stated:

> Whereas the spies and traitors known as the Royal Irish Constabulary are holding this country for the enemy, and whereas said spies and bloodhounds are conspiring with the enemy to bomb and bayonet and otherwise outrage a peaceful, law-abiding and liberty loving people; wherefore we hereby proclaim and suppress the said spies and traitors, and do hereby solemnly warn prospective recruits that they join the RIC at their own peril. All nations are agreed as to the fate of traitors. It has the sanction of God and man.[4]

As IRA attacks increased and the RIC began haemorrhaging men due to retirement and resignations, vulnerable police barracks in isolated rural areas were vacated and closed down. The term 'barracks' is usually associated with a military-type building, but the vast majority of RIC barracks were isolated buildings in rural areas, with no fortifications, or a two or three-storey terrace house in the middle of a small village. In larger barracks, the station sergeant would have had his family in residence. The barracks were in private, not state, ownership. By early 1920 the RIC had been forced to abandon over 500 of its barracks and drill halls in outlying areas, and in many parts of the country law and order virtually ceased to exist, with courts failing to sit and communications and general administration coming to a halt.

At the beginning of 1920 there were twenty-five police barracks in County Kildare. By March 1920 practically all of the barracks in the rural districts of the county had been vacated. Leixlip Barracks was closed down and its sergeant and four constables distributed to other stations. Castledermot and Ballitore Barracks suffered the same fate, with their men transferred to Athy, while Ballymore-Eustace Barracks was also closed down, its men going to Naas. Rathangan Barracks was closed in the first week of March. When Brownstown police station, on the edge of the Curragh was closed, there was no barracks nearer than Newbridge or Kildare town. This was situated on an important junction across the Curragh on the road from Newbridge to Kilcullen and to Kildare and Athy, with the result that closure led to a petition from the Curragh Camp to the Lord Lieutenant. The closure of Robertstown left that area one of the most exposed in the midlands, as there was no barracks closer than Naas or Celbridge.[5]

On Saturday night, 3–4 April, over 150 evacuated barracks were simultaneously burned throughout the country, together with income tax offices in sixteen different counties. In County Kildare, several vacated police barracks were ignited, including one at Lumville, less than a mile from the Curragh Camp, while the courthouse nearby was also destroyed. Simultaneously, Donadea, Ballinadrimna (Moyvalley), Clane, Ballitore and Kilteel Barracks were reduced to ruins by fire. The barracks were all empty with the exception of Clane, which was occupied by the wife of the sergeant during the day, although she and her children slept elsewhere at night. An attack on Carbury Barracks was unsuccessful, as the fire did not take hold. Kildare Volunteers also set fire to the barracks at Maynooth, Sallins, Kildoon, Castledermot, Ballymore-Eustace and Kill. Maynooth RIC Barracks had previously been closed for three weeks when instructions were issued for its reopening. The wife and family of the local sergeant were courteously ordered by the IRA to leave the barracks and were removed to another house, and the building was set alight. Motor cars crowded with cheering young men were seen driving away from the burning barracks. Six courthouses, including Donadea, were also burned. Large numbers of armed and disguised men arrived, spread paraffin oil or petrol and left hastily as the buildings went up in flames.[6] These operations proved, Lord French stated in an April interview with the *Daily Express* at the Viceregal Lodge in Dublin, that while the IRA did not show any evidence of military brains, there was no doubt of its organising power.[7]

Another concerted challenge to the authorities occurred on 5 April, when thirty-six untried republican prisoners in Mountjoy Jail went on hunger strike in a bid to force the British to recognise them as prisoners of war and not common criminals. Convicted republican prisoners who had been excluded from extra privileges soon joined them, bringing the total on the protest to ninety-two. The impact of the hunger strike outside Mountjoy was enormous. A general strike called in support of the hunger strikers on 13 April by the Labour Party brought most of the country to a standstill.[8] The strike coincided with the first day of the Punchestown race meeting, but it was decided to postpone it as the railways and other transport systems were also disrupted. Naas was crammed with race-goers, but when the postponement notice was published, the news of the general strike created consternation. Local IRA Volunteers were engaged in enforcing obedience to the strike order. Workers in Naas and the surrounding district for the most part ceased work in response to a call from the Trades Council. A procession of several hundred

St Patrick's Fife and Drum Band, 1921. *Back row (left to right):* J. Morrissey,
J. Gavin, M. Fitzpatrick, C. May, — Galloway. *Middle row:* P. Brophy,
M. Hannigan, B. Dunne, J. Fagan, M. Sheehan, T. Wilmot. *Front row:*
W. Smyth, M. Galloway, M. Hannigan, D. Meehan, A. Thopby, J. Angus.
Photo: Local Studies, Genealogy and Archives Dept, Newbridge Library

Cook and staff, Rath Camp, the Curragh, 1921.
Photo: Author's collection

The Rath Internment Camp, the Curragh, 1921.
Photo: Local Studies, Genealogy and Archives Dept, Newbridge Library

Kildare Fianna Éireann outside Naas Town Hall, on the way to
Bodenstown, *c.* 1918. Included in photo: P. Scanlon, T. Branagan,
B. Dempsey, T. Coyle, J. Dempsey, J. Dunne, B. Dillon, E. Grace,
J. Barry, M. Monaghan, J. Farrell, J. Dooley, L. Geraghty, P. Dowling,
H. Monaghan, J. Walsh, J. Sheehan.
Photo: Local Studies, Genealogy and Archives Dept, Newbridge Library

Left to right: Peter Traynor, Haynestown, Kill; Thomas McGivney, Dromahair, Co. Leitrim; Andy Farrell, Beggars End, Naas; John Traynor, Haynestown. Pictured outside Hut 1062, Rath Camp, 1921.
Photo: Paul Traynor

Curragh Camp West, *c.* 1910.
Photo: Local Studies, Genealogy and Archives Dept, Newbridge Library

Republican election group in Main Street, Naas, 1918 elections.
Photo: Stan Hickey

Parade ground of Naas Military Barracks, *c.* 1910.
Photo: Author's collection

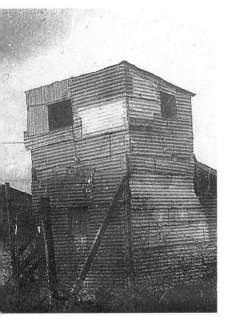

Guard tower at the Rath Camp, 1921.
Photo: Brid Hoey

Naas RIC Barracks.
Photo: Naas Local History Group

The Army and Navy Stores (second building from left), Ballymany, Newbridge, *c.* 1920. Burned down by the IRA on 7 July 1921, with two fatalities. *Photo: Author's collection*

Group of unidentified republican prisoners in the Rath Camp, 1921.
Photo: Brid Hoey

Pat Domican,
Kill Company, IRA.
Photo: Christy Domican

Domhnall Ua Buachalla, OC May-
nooth Company, who led a contingent
of Volunteers to Dublin, Easter 1916.
Photo: Adhamhnan Ó Súilleabháin

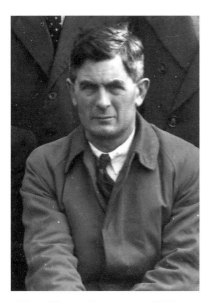

Tom Harris, Prosperous, Kildare
Brigade IRA 1914–21.
Photo: Aisling Dermody

Volunteer Joe Traynor, Haynestown, served with Kill Company,
IRA. *Photo: Paul Traynor*

FIRST EASTERN DIVISION.

GENERAL ORDER

9/7/21,

To, O/C. No. (7) ....*Naas*...... Brig.

    Owing to TRUCE been called at noon on MONDAY next, it is advisable
that a good stroke be made at the Enemy before then. Sucs stroke will it
is believed strenghten the hands of our representatives in the making of
a definite peace. You will therefore hit anywhere and everywhere you can
within your area before I2 NOON on MONDAY,
    The prinpipal objecti chould. in all cases be the members of old
R.I.C. or their Barracks.
    All SPIES of whom you may have already been advised off are to be
executed also before said hour on MONDAY.

        I M P O R T A N T

    It is to be definitely understood that all HOSTILITIESxxx cease
at I2 NOON on MONDAY THE IIth.OF JULY.

    Brig. Coms. have power in all cases to execute known SPIES or TRAIT@
-RS without consulting D.H.Q.
    In order to take advantage of terms of TRUCE and to prevent our O/C
from falling into hands of Enemy. The Div. meeting called for Monday
is hereby postponed until same hour on TUESDAY I2th. of July.
    Officers to report at Div. H.Q. on monday night.

        SIGNED DIV. ADJ.

Dispatch sent to 7th Brigade, First Eastern Division, prior to the Truce.
Photo: Author's collection

Comdt Michael Smyth, Athgarvan.
Photo: Cill Dara Historical Society

Ellen Gaul, *c.* 1920, a witness to many of the events in Naas during the War of Independence.
Photo: Author's collection

Thomas Carroll, Ballymore-Eustace, who served with the Dublin Brigade in the War of Independence.
Photo: Local Studies, Genealogy and Archives Dept, Newbridge Library

R. I. C.
Maynooth
6 March 1918

This is to certify that Mr. G. Brady
of Greenfield Maynooth requires to
enter the Co Clare in connection with
his business as a farmer + cattle
dealer,

P. Cleary
Const. in charge

RIC pass for G. Brady, Maynooth, 1918.
Photo: Local Studies, Genealogy and Archives Dept, Newbridge Library

people marched through the town to the Town Hall where they were addressed by republicans and trade unionists. The procession re-formed and continued to the local Catholic church, where a decade of the rosary was recited and answered in Irish by teachers and school children. The parish priest, Fr Norris, addressed the crowd, characterising their prayerful protest and procession 'as an admirable display of public sentiment on behalf of the suffering countrymen in Mountjoy'. Naas UDC also convened a special meeting to decide on a course of action to take in protest at the continued detention and treatment of the prisoners.

In Newbridge, the weekly fair was stopped as workers armed with hurleys guarded the roads leading into the town and prevented farmers from taking their livestock in. All shops were closed. There was a large procession to the Dominican church, where a special service for the prisoners was held. Afterwards local Labour leaders addressed a public meeting. In Monaster-evin, members of the Transport Workers' Union guarded the approaches to the town behind barbed wire entanglements to prevent the holding of the local fair.[9]

After Tom Ashe's death in 1917 a policy of 'no feeding, no release' had been tried, but proved unworkable. This new hunger strike left the government in an impossible situation. They could not force-feed the prisoners and could not let the strike reach its ultimate and fatal conclusion. The only solution was to release the untried prisoners. One of the released prisoners was Eamonn Malone from Barrowhouse, Athy. He was accorded an enthusiastic reception on his return home on 6 May 1920. Commandant Malone had spent twelve days on hunger strike in Mountjoy. His leadership qualities had been recognised by the republican prisoners there and he was elected to a three-man Prisoner's Council. When the hunger strike was decided upon, Malone was one of the first to volunteer. He was removed to Jervis Street Hospital when his condition deteriorated. An asthmatic for many years, Malone suffered ill health for the rest of his short life, no doubt brought on by the effects of hunger striking. As he stepped down from the train at Athy, he was cheered by the IRA Volunteers who had lined the station platform. Two republican bands led the procession through the town. The sidewalks were thronged with spectators and around 3,000 people crowded the Market Square. Michael Dooley, president of Athy Sinn Féin club, chaired the proceedings. Eamonn Malone addressed the crowd, thanking them for their support and urging them not to forget the rest of the prisoners in other prisons.[10]

In June there was a repeat performance of the March–April attacks on vacated barracks throughout the country. Such action showed a remarkable ability to co-ordinate a plan on a national level. Sallins RIC Barracks was attacked for the third time by the IRA, as the two previous attempts to destroy the building had failed – local residents extinguished the fires on one occasion. An estimated forty men took part in the operation: a large group of armed men arrived in the village on bicycles, while more armed men guarded the approach to the village. The raiders showed no fear of police arriving. This time the attackers made sure the operation would be successful by climbing onto the roof and breaking it in with pick-axes before pouring petrol into the building. Four men armed with revolvers also burned the signal cabin at Sallins railway station and took away official mail from the waiting-room.[11]

The Dunlavin Company, attached to Kildare Battalion, burned Ballitore, Dunlavin, Donard and Stratford-on-Slaney Barracks. They also attacked and occupied Baltinglass Barracks and killed one policeman. C Company, Castledermot, received orders to burn down the local police barracks, but when they arrived they found the sergeant's wife and family still in occupation. The men took the woman and her family to a neighbour's house and stored the furniture in a safe place. The building was sprinkled with petrol and in the resulting explosion one Volunteer was caught in a fireball. The unit's leader, Paddy Cosgrove, entered the burning building at great risk and brought him to safety. Cosgrove was so badly burned that the skin peeled off his face and hands, but he made a complete recovery in the hospital in Athy, where he was concealed and treated with the greatest care by the staff.[12]

On the same night, raids were carried out on customs offices in the county by County Kildare units attached to the Carlow and Laois battalions. All official documents were destroyed when the Kildare Town Company raided the local income tax office. Athy Company raided the local custom and excise office. Leixlip Company raided the rural district council offices in its area, while the excise officer's house near Naas was raided by a party of disguised and armed men, and large numbers of income tax papers and the keys of his office in Naas were confiscated. The raiders apologised for the inconvenience caused to the officer and his family. The excise office in Naas was then raided and more official papers taken. The premises of the County Kildare War Pensions Committee was also forcibly entered and many of the records burned.[13]

Naas Company was one of the most active Kildare units

during the war, with raids for arms in the district and the frequent stopping of the Sallins mail train.[14] When the RIC began to patrol Sallins rail station more regularly, the company went to nearby Straffan to conduct raids.

In May Dublin dockers had refused to handle any British war material. They were soon joined by the Irish Transport and General Workers' Union, which banned railway drivers from carrying British forces. When British soldiers or police boarded a train, the engine driver would refuse to start, leaving the military to drive. The railway men in Kildare were either members of the republican movement or strong supporters. On 1 June 1920 a meeting of railwaymen at Kildare town unanimously adopted a resolution that all railway employees were to refuse to handle all munitions or work on trains carrying troops. When a passenger train arrived at Newbridge from Kildare that evening, an officer tendered some rifles to the guard to be put on the train. The guard refused and the rifles had to be returned to the military barracks. The following morning a troop train arrived at Kildare station to convey troops and ammunition from Kildare to Athlone, but when the men arrived at the station the driver, fireman, guard and porters would have nothing to do with it. The troops had to return to their barracks in the Curragh, while the train remained in the station.[15] Eventually, train drivers were brought over from England. The rail strike pushed the military and police to rely on motor transport, which, of course, was more vulnerable to IRA attacks.

F Company, Kildare town, under Captain Denis O'Neill, was active on the Kildare railway line. As Kildare railway station was a junction, one line leading to Waterford and the other to Cork, it was an important centre for the distribution of communications from GHQ. Captain O'Neill and the company's first lieutenant were employed at the station and were in a good position to carry out this work. Raids were also made on trains for the British forces' mail and the station itself was raided. The IRA also raided mail trains at Newbridge and Sallins stations.

G Company, Monasterevin, was also active on the railways. When the railway men refused to drive trains carrying munitions or British military or police, they blocked the main Dublin to Cork road and the byroads around the town. They organised the collection of funds in the town for dismissed railway men. On one occasion Monasterevin Volunteers captured a consignment of five mailbags containing correspondence between the British Army and Dublin Castle at their local station. The captured bags were deemed so important that members of the brigade intelligence staff came to collect them.[16]

In August around 2,000 railway workers were dismissed from their employment country-wide due to their continued refusal to handle trains or railway wagons conveying arms or ammunition for the crown forces. The railway strike badly hampered British troop movements until 21 December 1920 when it was called off. Railwaymen acceded to the Labour Party's call to resume normal handling of government traffic as an alternative to the closure of the railways by the government. The British government threatened to withhold grants from the railway companies, which would have meant that workers would no longer be paid.[17]

During the local elections of county councils, rural district councils and boards of guardians in June, Kildare IRA men were engaged as guards at public meetings and at polling stations. The results, as expected, were an overwhelming victory for Sinn Féin.

The rural elections showed an even greater level of support for Sinn Féin than the January 1920 elections. The party took control of 338 out of 393 local government bodies, county councils, boards of guardians and rural district councils across the whole island. County council after county council declared its allegiance to Dáil Éireann, withholding payments of rates and taxes from the Local Government Board when practicable. At the Kildare County Council elections twenty-nine members were elected and twenty-eight of those were Sinn Féin or Labour. Only one Irish Parliamentary Party candidate was elected. The results for No. 1 Council, Naas Urban were 3 Sinn Féin; Naas Rural, 5 Sinn Féin; Newbridge, 3 Sinn Féin, 3 Labour; Athy, 3 Sinn Féin, 1 Labour; Kildare, 3 Sinn Féin, 2 Labour; Kilmeague, 4 Sinn Féin; Ballymore-Eustace, 1 Sinn Féin, 1 Labour; and Kilcullen, 4 Labour, 3 Sinn Féin.[18]

A *Kildare Observer* reporter was at the polling booth in a rural district in north Kildare where a woman entered to exercise her vote for the Naas No. 1 Rural District Council. She confessed to being illiterate, so the presiding officer asked her to whom she wished to give her first vote, to which she answered without hesitation. 'Your second?' queried the presiding officer, and again there was no hesitation. This continued until the woman had voted for five candidates. 'And your sixth?' said the presiding officer. 'Now,' said the harassed woman, 'I know you are trying to make fun of me. I thought I had only one vote when I came in, and you've taken five from me already. I'm only an ignorant woman with one vote and if you're not satisfied with all I've given, then give them back to me and let me about my business!'[19]

At the first Kildare County Council meeting in Naas, on 21

June 1920, it was decided to pledge allegiance to Dáil Éireann and to repudiate any claim by the British to legislate in Irish affairs. The chairman elected was Domhnall Ua Buachalla – a post he held until 1922 – while republicans Michael Smyth and Thomas Harris were also members of the council. Éamon Ó Modhrain was elected vice-chairman. Every effort was made by the British to compel the council, and indeed councils nationwide, to recognise the British Local Government Board, including the issuing of writs.

The new council deleted the resolutions condemning the Easter Rising passed by Kildare County Council in 1916 from the minutes. Proposed by Councillor Michael Smyth (Labour) and seconded by Hugh Colohan: 'That the resolution passed unanimously in May 1916, condemning the Rebellion of Easter week be deleted from the minutes of the Council.' In the following weeks resolutions were also passed concerning the treatment of Irish political prisoners, proposing the release of Jim Larkin and in support of the railwaymen and dockers refusing to handle munitions.

The interest of the new members of the county council in the Irish language was demonstrated in the publication of the council's proceedings in both Irish and English in the *Leinster Leader*. Naas Urban District Council and the Newbridge Town Commissioners showed a similar interest in the language in the autumn of that year when both bodies, dominated by Sinn Féin, proposed that the names of their towns should be changed to the Gaelic forms. The proposals were adopted at the quarterly meeting of Kildare County Council on 22 November and henceforth the towns were to be known as Nas Ni Riogh and Droichead Nua.[20]

The Celbridge No. 1 District Council, Mr M. Fay presiding,

decided unanimously at the July monthly meeting that no lists of ratepayers for the information of 'British agents' would be drawn up in the council office, nor any facilities given for copying or taking extracts from rate or valuation books for such purposes; that no lists would be supplied to such agents showing the salaries or wages paid by the council to officials or employees; that every possible obstacle would be placed in the way of the British government for collecting taxes or otherwise; and that where at all possible only Irish goods would be purchased by the council.[21]

By the early summer the IRA had achieved a measure of success in clearing the RIC from smaller Irish villages and towns. As soon as a barracks was abandoned, they burned it or rendered it uninhabitable, so that by the end of June 1920, 351 evacuated barracks had been destroyed, with a further 105 damaged. Fifteen occupied barracks were also destroyed, along with twenty-five damaged. From the twenty-four RIC barracks in County Kildare at the beginning of the year, only six were active at the end of August.[22] The closure of these rural barracks left whole areas of the country under republican control. As it became necessary for the police to patrol in bigger groups, this could only be done from the larger barracks where the personnel were available. The only way the police could travel was by motor vehicle. The RIC acquired Leyland and Crossley tenders, which could carry up to twelve men, and these became their most common forms of transport. To obstruct the RIC's travel, the IRA trenched roads, leaving a margin that would allow a farm cart to pass beside a trench, but into which a tender or lorry travelling at high speed would crash. By this time over 1,000 Black and Tans had been distributed throughout the country to strengthen police posts, while others were on their way, to make, in the words of the *Dublin Police Journal*, 'Ireland hell for rebels to live in'.[23]

Rioting broke out in Belfast in late July after the assassination of RIC Divisional Commander Gerald Bryce Ferguson Smyth in Cork. Smyth, who had ordered his men to 'shoot on sight' people with their hands in their pockets approaching police, was shot dead by the IRA in the Cork County Club. With him was Naas-born County Inspector George Craig, who was wounded in the leg. The assassins were not masked and one asked Smyth, 'Were not your orders to shoot at sight? Well, you are in sight now, so prepare.' After Smyth's funeral in Banbridge, County Down, loyalists attacked Catholics in Banbridge and Belfast, which resulted in seven deaths and over 100 people injured. In retaliation the Dáil introduced a boycott on Belfast businesses and manufacturers, despite opposition from Ernest Blythe, the sole Ulster Protestant member.[24]

On 20 July IRA Volunteers burned the courthouse at Athy. The building, situated in Emily Square adjacent to the Town Hall, was completely consumed by fire. Also in July an IRA training camp was established at Ladytown, Naas, under the charge of Peadar McMahon, and was attended by officers from all companies in the North Kildare Battalion area. An intensive training course was carried out. G Company, Monasterevin, was also active in the Curragh area, blowing up a bridge over the River Barrow and destroying a local excise office and British cargo being transported by canal. However, the company was dealt a severe blow when Captain Hugh McNally and Quartermaster Fintan Brennan were captured in a raid by military and police, along with most of the company's equipment. Captain McNally was sentenced to ten years' and Brennan to five years' penal servitude.[25]

In both Britain and Ireland criminal cases were tried quarterly. The summer assizes were held in Ireland in June and July 1920. For the British government the results were disastrous. Sir Hamar Greenwood, the Chief Secretary for Ireland, told the cabinet that 'throughout the greater part of Ireland criminal justice can no longer be administered by the ordinary constitutional process of trial by judge and jury'.[26] Security was heavy for the sitting in County Kildare in late July – the judges were escorted from their hotel to Naas courthouse while police and military patrolled the streets.

The Irish Times, considered the paper of record for historians and researchers, contained a daily summary of outrages reported from every district in the country. The summary of official reports of outrages received on 20 July 1920, contained the following:

Co. Kildare – At 12.30 p.m. on the 19th a rural postman was held up between Rathangan and Clonbealogue, Kildare district, by two armed and masked men, who searched the mails. On the morning of the 18th Ballymore-Eustace vacated R.I.C. barrack, Naas district, was maliciously set on fire and completely destroyed. The courthouse was also set on fire and partially destroyed, and the books and records were taken out and burned.[27]

The summary received on 21 July contained the following:

Co. Kildare – At 2.30 a.m. on the 20th Castledermot vacated police barracks, Athy district, was maliciously burned. The courthouse, which was situated about ten yards from the barrack, was also destroyed by fire. The sub-standards of weights and measures and a number of books were also destroyed. Three telegraph wires were also cut outside the village. At 2 a.m. on the 20th the vacated R.I.C. barrack at Nurney, Kildare district, was set on fire and completely destroyed.[28]

On 24 July it was reported that the county of Kildare was in 'a deplorable state':

The County Kildare Assizes opened at Naas Courthouse on the morning of 23 July 1920. Police and infantry guarded the Hotel at which the Judges stayed. Lancers patrolled all the streets, while an infantry picket was placed in front of the courthouse. The Lord Chief Justice, addressing the Grand Jury, said there were nine cases to go before them. He was sorry to tell them that the general condition of the county must be described as bad. There had only been nineteen cases in 1919, but so far in 1920 they had increased to ninety. There were three facts in which consolation might be derived, the Chief Justice declared: that there had been no loss of life, that the increase in number of specially reported cases had been far exceeded in other counties, and that the number of persons made amenable through the vigilance of the police had been greater than in other counties. After making every allowance and giving all the consolation he could, the returns before him exhibited a deplorable state of affairs. In the last four months there had been twenty-eight cases of arson, involving the destruction of as many police barracks, courthouses, and other property; some eighteen cases of burglary, house-breaking, and robbery; fourteen cases of malicious injury, unaccompanied by arson; eleven cases of larceny of various kinds, and nine cases of threatening letters. The remainder was composed of assaults, raids for arms and documents, and other things. The mad craving for destruction had fallen on income tax papers and Sunday papers (burned, he supposed, because they came from England). He was unable to find any explanation why papers belonging to the War Pensions Committee should be burned as they had been in their county. The attacks on barracks and courthouses extended to signal cabins on the railway – a mad and futile sort of crime that might involve loss of many lives. The greatest danger confronting the people, the Lord Chief Justice said, was the weakening of the moral law, which, unless grappled with successfully, would undo the good work of centuries and leave Ireland poor indeed.[29]

As the pace of the war in Dublin and certain areas of the country increased considerably, local men continued to resign or retire from the RIC. In Kildare, because of the low level of attacks on the police, only about eight men resigned. In other parts of the country it was different. There were 556 Irish resignations from the RIC between 1 May and 31 July 1920. Their places were taken by over 800 Black and Tan recruits. The British government refused to concede that there was actually a war in progress in Ireland, as claimed by the IRA, and in strengthening the police rather than the military, they could justify 'the Troubles' as mere 'civil disorder'.

To further augment the strength of the RIC and the Black and Tans, a new group of English recruits arrived in Ireland in late July. They were the Auxiliary Division, who quickly became known as the 'Auxies', though they referred to themselves as 'Tudor's Toughs' after Major-General Sir Henry Hugh Tudor, Inspector General of the RIC. The Auxies were ex-officers who had served overseas. They were paid £1 a day, plus cost-of-living expenses, for their service in Ireland. They wore their own distinctive dark blue uniform and Glengarry-style caps – Tam O'Shanters and later Balmorals. Their title was temporary constable or cadet and they were distinct from the RIC. Based in Dublin and in the most troublesome spots around the country, they earned a reputation for ruthlessness and bravery. Many had been awarded bravery medals arising from service in the First World War and in time they became more feared than the Black and Tans.

Like the Black and Tans, the new recruits received a six-week training course in the Curragh Camp, where conditions were poor. Brigadier General Francis P. Crozier was appointed commandant of the Auxiliary Division. According to him:

> A lot of misery, inconvenience, and hard drinking could have been avoided had arrangements been made for the reception of these men, for their ordinary comfort – quartering, messing, and discipline – but instead the men were running about the Curragh as they liked. The original members of the Division, which then had no name, had to arrange their own messing and canteens, and there was nobody in command.[30]

Due to disciplinary matters, and possibly inter-regimental rivalry with the regular military, Crozier had the training centre transferred to Beggar's Bush, Dublin, where a dedicated training camp was established for the new temporary constables/cadets. He resigned from his post early the next year over controversial issues relating to discipline in the Auxiliary Division and was subsequently severely critical of the British conduct of affairs in Ireland.[31]

The Restoration of Order Bill introduced in August 1920 gave Dublin Castle the power to govern by regulation, to replace the criminal courts with courts martial, to replace coroner's inquests with military courts of inquiry and to punish disaffected local governments by withholding grants of money.

Despite the raids, burnings and general lawlessness of the county, the editor of *The Kildare Observer* claimed that in the month of August 'the people of Kildare had reason to congratulate themselves on the fact that the county had remained quite free from any crime causing loss of life arising out of the disturbed state of the country generally'.[32] By this stage there were two IRA battalions in Kildare, composed of eighteen companies of about 300 men, but only about 100 of these were available at any given time to take to the field. There had been little confrontation with the RIC or military, but that was to change on the night of 21 August 1920.[33]

On that night Commandant Tom Harris led the Kill Company in an attack on a police patrol near Naas. Since the attack on Inspector Supple's home on the Sallins Road, the previous January, by Naas Company, a patrol of four policemen left Kill Barracks every second night to stand guard. Scouts observed the policemen's routine and on information received Captain Pat Dunne, Kill, decided to ambush the police on the Monread Road, near Naas. When Dunne was taken ill, Harris took command of the attack. Commandant Pat Colgan, Maynooth, sent two boxes of cartridges for the Volunteers' shotguns.[34] Around 11 p.m. on 21 August four policemen – Sergeant O'Reilly and Constables Haverty, Flanagan and Flaherty – left the barracks at Kill to cycle to Naas. As they approached a small plantation at

Greenhills, half a mile from Kill, they heard a shout of 'Hands Up!' According to the evidence of one of the survivors of the ambush, they did not have time to react, as a volley of shots accompanied the shout. All four men fell from their bicycles and were immediately surrounded by a large group of men, who levelled weapons at them.[35] Jim Dunne was present at the ambush and left this account:

On the 15th August, 1920, Captain P. Dunne returned from Battalion Training Centre, suffering from a chill on the kidneys and was confined to bed under doctor's care. He sent word to Commandant Colgan to postpone the ambush until he was up again, but as plans were so far advanced Colgan decided to send Thomas Harris to take charge. The whole Kill Company of 33 men were called out to take part and mobilised under Thomas Domican, 1st Lieutenant. We were instructed to wear masks. The ambush position was changed from Monread Road to main Naas/Dublin road at Greenhills, Kill, and the date was 20th [sic] August, 1920. The main body of about 20 men, with ten shotguns and some revolvers, were placed behind a bank beside the main road with a small wood or screen with trees at their back. I was sent with five men under Jack Sullivan, Section Commander, to the Kill side of the main body, with instructions to close up behind the police patrol and not to allow any of them to get back to barracks, which was only a ¼ mile away, and at the same time to watch out for enemy convoys travelling the main road. Only myself and Sullivan were armed. I had a shotgun and Sullivan had a Colt 38 Automatic.

William Daly, Section Commander, was in charge of the advance guard on Naas side of ambush position with five men, two armed, to stop police if any escaped in that direction. Three more men were behind the main body with the extra ammunition.

About 10.30 p.m. a cycle patrol of four police appeared, riding singly about 20 yards apart. We let the last R.I.C. man pass and closed up at about 100 yards behind. When the first R.I.C. man, a Sergeant, neared the end of the main body, he was called on to halt. He said, 'All right, men.' When Tom and Pat Domican jumped from behind the ditch, he opened fire on them. General firing broke out along the main body of Volunteers. At the time, I, with Sullivan, was close up to the rere of the police. Two of them attempted to escape back to barracks and were captured by myself and Sullivan. P. Brady, although unarmed, rushed in and disarmed the two police, whom we took prisoners. The other two R.I.C. men were killed in the first volley. All the arms and ammunition were collected and given to unarmed Volunteers to dump. Myself, Sullivan and Brady then marched the captured police to Palmerstown Estate, 300 yards away, and instructed them not to report to barracks until the morning.

The whole operation was over in 20 minutes, as there was grave danger of enemy convoys travelling the main road and from 100 police and 400 soldiers stationed at Naas, three miles away, and from 20 police in Kill, ¼ mile away, who could be on the spot within a half hour.

None of our men were wounded. Men of the main body of Volunteers who were armed were: 1st Lieutenant T. Domican, P. Domican, P. Magee, Peter Traynor, John Traynor, Patrick Kelly, Jer Kelly, Tom Nolan and J. Kelly (Kilteel). Captured material – two .45 revolvers, 2 carbine rifles and a large store of ammunition.

Tom Harris returned to Prosperous after the ambush as it was too risky to remain in the Kill area. His revolver was dumped by my brother, Dick, who was with W. Daly's section.

After the ambush, the police and troops combed the area but did not succeed in capturing any of our men, who had to go 'on the run'.[36]

The two policemen killed were Sergeant Patrick O'Reilly and Constable John Haverty of Kill Barracks. Sergeant O'Reilly was taken to Steeven's Hospital, Dublin, where he died on 31 August. Constable Haverty was shot through the chest and died immediately. Reilly (48) was a married man from King's County (Offaly), who had twenty-six years' service in the RIC and was due to retire in three weeks. Haverty (40) was single and from Ballinasloe, County Galway, with nineteen years' service. Constable Flanagan, one of the survivors, resigned a week later, after seven years' service.[37]

On 26 August, Broughall's public house in Kill, The Dew Drop Inn, was visited by a party of twenty policemen armed with rifles and revolvers. The inn was directly opposite the RIC barracks. A lorry carrying the policemen drove up to the pub and parked nearby. Two policemen, one in uniform trailing a rifle and the other in civilian clothes with a drawn revolver, went inside. One RIC man shouted, 'What bastard killed the policeman? Will anyone kill one tonight?' The other approached the counter and demanded two pints of ale from Mrs Broughall, whose husband and assistant, just back from haymaking, were upstairs. As she was putting the pints on the counter, the man in civilian clothes fired two shots from his revolver into the ceiling. Terror-stricken, Mrs Broughall ran out the door as the civilian-clad policeman shouted, 'We'll blow up this place tonight.' They took away large amounts of liquor and destroyed the remaining bottles, firing shots at some and smashing the rest on the floor. The rest of the police assisted them. While this was going on a policeman drew his revolver and shot and killed a mare in a nearby field. They then departed, cheering and shouting.

Another party of police arrived and caused more damage to The Dew Drop Inn. They had a list of names and told men on the premises, 'Get out home, we don't want any of you.' Mr Broughall then arrived and closed the pub. Between midnight and 2 a.m. more police and military arrived in Kill village and searched the house of a known republican, throwing bedclothes into the yard. A local man returning home late was severely assaulted by one of the raiders. Several houses, including the home of the Domican brothers, were raided and some items taken away.

Two lorries with ten policemen in each arrived in Naas that same night between midnight and 1 a.m. from the Curragh direction. The lorries drove up Basin Street. One parked at the Town Hall and the other at Staples Dowlings' public house, on the corner of Basin Street. Fortunately, no inhabitants were on the street at the time. People were woken by sustained firing for about ten minutes from the Black and Tans, who were in open formation across the street. Loud knocking was heard at the door of Whyte's drapery, then the sound of breaking glass. The premises of Boushell's Family Boot Maker and Leather Merchant at South Main Street went up in flames. Mr and Mrs Boushell had to escape by a back entrance. The police left, firing revolvers and rifles. Shortly afterwards two Very lights, or flares, were fired from the police barracks and the town's inhabitants came out to try to stop the flames spreading to the nearby *Leinster Leader* office. Despite their efforts, Boushell's was completely destroyed. Cartridges, whiskey bottles and two RIC caps were later found in the street. As the police headed out the Limerick Road they fired a volley into the residence of James Dowling, Barrack Gate, and bullets also hit several houses nearby. Fortunately, no one was injured.[38]

Ellen Mahon, née Gaul, recalled that the reason Boushell's was burned down was that a party of Black and Tans, probably from the Curragh, were looking for the home of local republican Jimmy Whyte, who lived on the opposite side of Main Street (now Haydes shop), and, acting on incorrect information, torched Boushell's by mistake. This was the general consensus for the arson attack. However, the late Peter Lawler, a prominent local republican, maintained that when a detachment of Black and Tans first arrived in Naas, Bernard Boushell cleared out his shop window leaving only two shoes in public view. One shoe was black and the other tan! The Black and Tans probably did not forget this slight and torched Boushell's at the first opportunity.[39] It is also possible that they could not find Jimmy Whyte's home and so they decided to burn the next best thing.

A special meeting of Naas UDC was called on 27 August to 'express the abhorrence of the members at the conduct of the armed forces of the British Government at Naas last night, in the burning and destruction of the house of Bernard Boushell, and the indiscriminate firing into the homes of the people in the dead hours of the night'. The *Leinster Leader* of 28 August stated:

Amongst those who assisted in extinguishing the fire were the following – County Inspector K. L. Supple, Major Foley, D. I., and the local police. Messers P. Byrne, M. Cush, P. F. Grehan, M. Fitzsimons, W. O'Brien, John Sheridan, Mr. Treacy, J. Grehan, W. Whyte, J. Fennessy, J. O'Neill, M. Farrell, J. Farrell, J. Rafferty, W. McCormack, and numerous other residents who worked with a will for several hours. The ruins were still smouldering on Friday morning. Three of those who persisted in extinguishing the fire are ex-soldiers.

During the War of Independence it was quickly forgotten that many of the RIC casualties were fellow Irishmen, neighbours and co-religionists. The removal of Constable Haverty's remains took place from Kill Barracks the following Tuesday morning to Sallins station, where they were entrained to his native place for interment. The chief mourners were the deceased's aging father and two brothers. A number of beautiful wreaths were placed upon the coffin. Messages of sympathy were received from the Lord Lieutenant and the Inspector General RIC. Rev. John Donovan, PP, Kill, received a letter from the Most Rev. Dr Foley, Bishop of Kildare and Leighlin, strongly condemning the attack as an 'awful crime'.[40]

The *Leinster Leader* duly reported on the follow-up raids by the police and military in the Kill area for men wanted in connection with the ambush, while the IRA in Naas were busy raiding for arms:

On Friday last in Naas and district there were several raids by civilians for arms. Shotguns, rifles, and revolvers with ammunition are reported to have been carried away. It would appear that in each case the raiders promised that the arms would be well cared for and returned to the owners as soon as possible. Reports would indicate that there was nothing in the way of opposition offered to the raiders and that in each case the arms asked for were handed over. It is stated that in each case the raiders acted courteously and apologised for any trouble they had caused. A large number of arms were secured from all over the district. It is stated that the Royal Irish Constabulary have been active in collecting arms in the district for which the owners held permits.

Armed police under the command of officers visited on

Friday last the district of Kill, the scene of the recent ambush of an RIC patrol when a sergeant and a constable were shot dead. Several houses were raided and subjected to a very close search, but no arrests were made. Amongst the houses searched were those of Mr. John Traynor, Co. C., RDC, Woolpack, and Mr. T. Domican, RDC, Kill.

We have been informed that while Mr Patrick Dunne, Greenhills, Kill, was conversing near his home with two young men named Domican, a number of RIC men in charge of an officer arrived in a motor lorry. They approached and seized the two Domicans, and subjected them to a search, during which a sergeant tore the buttons from the clothes of one of them. They complain that before departing the RIC officer in charge used abusive language, and indulged in threats against their lives, in certain eventualities, and that they are prepared to substantiate these statements if afforded an opportunity.[41]

There were two other fatal attacks in County Kildare involving the police – in Maynooth an RIC man was killed and in Barrowhouse, near Athy, two IRA Volunteers were slain. Both incidents led to reprisals on the local population, which acted as a deterrent against further attacks.

The Greenhills ambush and its subsequent reprisals in Naas and Kill by the Black and Tans were the norm during the War of Independence. While not downplaying their effect on the local population, the crown forces' attacks in Naas and Kill were very tame compared with those in Munster and other parts of the country, where the war, and subsequent reprisals, were more severe.

At the end of August Celbridge IRA burned down the police barracks and the courthouse. Celbridge had been made a special constabulary centre when the different barracks in Maynooth, Kilcock, Leixlip, Clane and Robertstown were closed. The men from these districts were drafted into the Celbridge area, where there was a large barracks overlooking the Liffey. The barracks was heavily fortified against attack but a tactical decision was taken to evacuate it early on the morning of 30 August, possibly to the more easily defended barracks in nearby Lucan, County Dublin. The following morning a large body of men arrived by motor and bicycle and proceeded to burn the barracks and the courthouse.[42]

In September there were several resignations from the police and judiciary in Kildare. Constable Barrett, a veteran of the First World War and a native of Cork, was dismissed from the RIC at Monasterevin for refusing to do 'certain' duty. In Naas, two constables resigned from the force. Six local county JPs also resigned their Commissions of the Peace. IRA activity was heightened in the first week of September as Volunteers raided ninety-two houses in the county for guns.[43]

On 29 September a car containing three plainclothes policemen knocked down and killed a civilian riding a motorbike towards Newbridge at Newhall, Naas. Edward Nolan, a driver and collector for a Dublin firm, was hit by the Crossley tender 'travelling at a dangerous speed'. He had been awarded the OBE (Order of the British Empire) for his work as an ambulance man during the Easter Rising. The men, who were attached to the RIC Depot, Phoenix Park, Dublin, seemed to be lost and were looking for a back road to Carlow near Newhall. They alighted from their vehicle, apparently nervous, with revolvers drawn and held up several civilians travelling on the road. Nolan's body was brought back to Naas by the local RIC. Only the driver appeared at the inquiry.[44]

Heavy military and police raids took place in the Athy area during September and October 1920, and the Gaelic League rooms in Kildoon were burned down by persons unknown. In Athy, the military and police arrived in force on 4 September. Two lorry loads of infantry descended on the town and after forming up in the lane near the police barracks assembled at Emily Square, they used searchlights on the surrounding area. The troops raided a house in Offaly Street and took away a photograph of a wanted man – money, food and a razor were also taken – and a public house on the quay was thoroughly searched for a named assistant. Two nights later two lorry loads of military and police on bicycles arrived in the town. One of the lorries struck a lamp post, tearing it from its foundation and strewing the wreckage around the road. Having escorted the police to the barracks, the lorries drove off.

The situation in and around Kill in September and October was similar. The houses of persons believed to be sympathetic to the republican movement were subjected to exhaustive searches, including outhouses and haystacks. Amongst the houses raided was that of Thomas Domican, and the police made inquiries for Tom and Pat Domican, neither of whom were at home. The house was searched from top to bottom and the raiders tore up pictures and photos of republican interest, destroyed a bicycle and took food. In another house the raiders destroyed a suit of clothes. Mr Broughall's licensed premises in Kill and the local ITGWU Hall were also raided and searched. On the following day the house of Patrick Dunne, Greenhills, was raided and the subject of a close search. The raiders also visited the house of John Traynor,

Woolpack, and inquired for him and his brothers, who were not at home – Mrs Traynor, her daughter and another woman were the only occupants. The house was thoroughly searched and left in a state of disorder. When leaving, one of the raiders said they would return when Traynor and his brothers were at home.[45]

Raids continued throughout the county: houses in Kilcock and district were searched and when the raiders failed to find the man for whom they inquired, they cut up his Sunday clothes and boots; two machine guns were set up on the street at Johnstownbridge while troops raided a licensed premises. In Kildare town, George Graham, a farmer and owner of a bakery and confectionary shop in the town, was shot and seriously wounded as he drove past the military barracks. The military claimed to have issued a warning before opening fire on Graham's car, but he claimed to have heard nothing other than what he thought were 'squibs being let off'. Two bullets struck Graham in the back and chest. Luckily, his son, who was travelling with him, was uninjured. George Graham made a full recovery.[46]

In October Captain Pat Dunne of Kill Company asked Commandant Harris to allow him to start a 'flying column' in the Kill area, as he had up to a dozen men on the run. Harris replied that he had instructions from GHQ that a column in the Kill area would cut the line of communication to the south of the country, which had to be kept open for dispatches. Kill Company was reduced to blocking roads, raiding post offices and training. However, owing to these activities, the RIC holding Kilteel Barracks were withdrawn to Naas RIC Barracks. The twenty-two police stationed at Kill had already withdrawn to Naas. Kill Company subsequently burned the abandoned Kilteel Barracks;

the withdrawal of the RIC left the countryside around Kill and Kilteel in the hands of the IRA.

The RIC and British troops swept large areas around Kill and Kilteel in an effort to capture IRA men on the run. These men were nearly always warned of approaching raids by the wife of RIC Sergeant Minihan, and by Sergeant Jeremiah Maher in Naas Barracks. However, in the months of October and November the authorities picked up thirteen men of the Kill Company, including Captain Dunne, who was arrested with Lieutenant Tom Domican when they were visiting the daughter of Captain Dunne, who was terminally ill (she died three days later).[47] Both were at first held in the Curragh. Dunne was court-martialled for being in possession of arms and sentenced to nine months' imprisonment in Mountjoy Jail.

On 1 November eighteen-year-old Kevin Barry was hanged in Mountjoy Jail for his part in an attack on British troops in Dublin and an ambush was arranged on the same day for Newbridge railway station. Tom Harris, Michael Smyth and Seán Kavanagh were among the men who mobilised for the ambush on an expected party of soldiers, but the military party failed to turn up and the attack never materialised. Maureen Cusack recalled how her father-in-law, J. P. Cusack, who was imprisoned in Mountjoy at the time, said that the inmates booed the warders and hangman who led Barry to the scaffold. That week Naas UDC proposed a vote of sympathy to the family of Kevin Barry and adjourned their meeting.[48]

On 18 November James Collins, Intelligence Officer, Kilcullen Company, called with several Volunteers, to a house at Knockbounce, Kilcullen, to settle a family feud. Shots had earlier been fired into the house. The RIC also had information on the matter and seven policemen were waiting at the gate of the house. They called on the Volunteers to halt. The IRA shone two bicycle lamps on the RIC and allegedly fired on them. The RIC returned fire and Thomas Hazlett and William Martin were wounded. Five more republicans were arrested in the vicinity and brought to Kilcullen RIC Barracks. The wounded men were taken to Kildare County Infirmary. The RIC claimed there were up to fifteen Volunteers at Knockbounce at the time in marching order, though no arms or ammunition were found. The arrested Volunteers, excluding Collins, were charged with aiding other persons unknown in discharge of firearms, whereby members of the RIC were endangered. However, they were found not guilty of all charges and released.[49]

On Sunday 21 November the RIC raided the courthouse in Naas and seized the county council's records. Several members of the council were arrested.[50] That same morning – less than two weeks after Lloyd George declared at the lord mayor's banquet in London, 'We have murder by the throat!' – a select group of men from the Dublin Brigade, augmented by Squad members, converged on several residences in Dublin and shot dead fourteen suspected British agents who had recently arrived in the city to smash Michael Collins' intelligence system. Despite the unease in the city after the morning's killings, some 15,000 spectators attended Croke Park to see Dublin play Tipperary in a Gaelic football challenge match. The challenge match, arranged in aid of the Republican Prisoners' Dependants' Fund, was between the two top football teams at the time. Both counties took the challenge seriously and full-strength teams were selected. Frank

Bourke of Carbury was playing left corner forward for Dublin. He was a teacher in St Enda's and played club football for Dublin side Collegians. Dublin lined out in county colours, while Tipperary wore the green and white colours of Grangemockler.[51] The referee was Mick Sammon, from Mainham, Clane.

Sammon threw in the ball at 2.45 p.m.: the whistle he used is still cherished by family members.[52] Shortly afterwards an aeroplane flew over the ground and a flare was shot from the cockpit to signal that the match was on. A detachment of Auxiliaries and regular troops arrived at the ground at 3.15. They divided into four groups and occupied each corner of the field. An officer on top of a wall fired a revolver shot. Stationed at a railway bridge at one end of the ground, a group of Auxiliaries fired a machine gun at random into the crowd. The crowd thought at first they were firing blanks, but as the fire increased in volume the spectators stampeded towards the railway wall, furthest from the gunfire. One player, Michael Hogan of Tipperary, was shot through the head as he jumped for the ball. Another Tipperary player, Jim Egan, was wounded. A young man who attempted to whisper an Act of Contrition into the dying Hogan's ear was also shot dead. The *Leinster Leader* reporter stated that he had earlier spoken to Hogan and crawled along the sideline when the gunfire started.

People panicked and ran onto the pitch. More shots were fired and dead and wounded were scattered around. The presence of the military probably saved many more innocent people from being killed. A drunken Auxiliary lined up the two teams and walked up and down in front of them, a revolver in his hand, muttering threats and curses. An army officer approached the Auxie and persuaded him to leave. Twelve people were killed and around seventy wounded. The casualties included Jeannie Boyle, who was due to be married five days later, and fourteen-year-old John Scott, so mutilated that it was thought he had been bayoneted to death.[53] The British authorities released the following statement:

> A number of men came to Dublin on Saturday under the guise of asking to attend a football match between Tipperary and Dublin. But their real intention was to take part in a series of murderous outrages, which took place in Dublin that morning. Learning on Saturday that a number of these gunmen were present in Croke Park, the Crown forces went to raid the field. It was the original intention that an officer would go to the centre of the field and speak from a megaphone, invite the assassins to come forward. But on their approach, armed pickets gave warning. Shots were fired to warn the wanted men, who caused a stampede and escaped in the confusion.[54]

However, one of the Auxiliaries involved in the operation recalled that they tossed a coin over whether they would go on a killing spree in Croke Park or loot Sackville Street instead.[55]

That night Auxiliaries killed three IRA men picked up in raids that morning. They were shot dead while allegedly 'trying to escape'. Casualties for that day, which became known as 'Bloody Sunday', amounted to sixteen members of the crown forces, sixteen civilians and three IRA men killed, and nearly 100 civilians and military wounded. One civilian injured in Croke Park died of wounds later that week.[56]

The immediate British response after Bloody Sunday was to resort to internment on an unprecedented scale and an overall intensification of the counter-insurgency drive. Eight hundred

Volunteers were picked up in country-wide sweeps. Tom Traynor, Woolpack, Kill, was arrested in a general round-up in Wexford and interned at Cork Jail. He had already served six months in Cork for wearing a Volunteer uniform. Two days after Bloody Sunday RIC Sergeant McGowan of Newbridge Barracks passed on information that there was to be an intensive campaign of raids by the crown forces in County Kildare the following week. Although Volunteers were warned not to sleep at home, some did and their houses were surrounded in the early hours of the morning and they were arrested. Ten houses were raided in Kildare town and four lorry loads of Black and Tans made general searches in Athy. Among those picked up in the raids were Adjutant Seán Curry and OC Tom Patterson, Naas; John Traynor, Kill; Captain Tom Dunne, Newbridge; and Commandant No. 2 Kildare Battalion, Tom Harris.[57]

As British raids intensified, Eamonn Malone, OC Carlow Brigade, was also picked up. He was OC of the brigade from 1917 up to his arrest in November 1920. The only son of a Cork University professor, Malone had returned with his mother to Barrowhouse, Athy, on the death of his father and joined the Irish Volunteers. He went on the run after the 'German Plot' and moved from safe house to safe house, never staying more than one night in any one place. On 27 November he was at 41 Duke Street, Athy, the home of a known republican, Michael Dooley. While moving to another location in Woodstock Street, in the company of another local republican, Joe May, they were spotted by the wife of a local RIC man, who promptly informed the authorities. Joe May's house in Woodstock Street was raided by Black and Tans from nearby Ballylinan and he was arrested and brought to the Curragh Camp. May was detained in the Curragh for three weeks before being transferred to Arbour Hill and then to Ballykinlar Camp, County Down. Eamonn Malone escaped as he was staying several houses away, but was arrested a few days later.[58]

The arrests of so many top men in the week after Bloody Sunday led to the re-formation of Kildare 2nd Battalion Council as follows: Commandant, Michael Smyth; Vice-Commandant, Art Doran; Adjutant and Intelligence Officer, Seán Kavanagh; Quartermaster, James Harris. New company officers were also appointed in place of those arrested. Michael Smyth immediately received a 'death notice' from the 'forces of law and order', dated 1 December 1920:

FINAL WARNING

Whereas, it has come to our knowledge that the Sinn Fein organisation of which you are a prominent official through the so-called IRA or murder gang has been committing outrages in this hitherto God-fearing and law-abiding country, this reign of terror must be stopped. You are, therefore, most earnestly warned that in the event of the continuance of those heartless and cowardly crimes you will be personally held responsible and punished in such a manner that others will be deterred from criminal course.

By order.

Michael Smyth,
Athgarvan, Newbridge,
Co. Kildare.[59]

In early December there was an unsuccessful attack on Kilcullen RIC Barracks by men of the 6th Carlow Battalion, in which the 2nd Kildare Battalion co-operated by blocking all roads between Kilcullen and the Curragh Camp. Kilcullen Company was attached to the 6th Carlow Battalion. The company area bordered the Curragh Camp and their chief activities were blocking and trenching roads leading to the camp. Cutting the telephone wires also caused disruption to British communications.

In Naas, on 23 December, shots were fired by the RIC as they raided the Workingman's Club, the Sinn Féin Hall and Hibernian Hall, all in the Main Street. The area was surrounded and everyone inside the buildings was searched and told to keep their hands up. No arms were found or arrests made, though several houses in the town were also searched.[60]

As 1920 closed, the British parliament passed the Government of Ireland Act, which provided for the partition of Ireland. There was to be a crown colony government in Belfast to govern six Ulster counties and a dominion government in Dublin to rule the remaining twenty-six counties, with elections to take place early in the following year. The timing of the elections obviously depended on the overall military situation. By this time the Belfast boycott was starting to have an effect. Due to the enforcement of the boycott started in August by the IRA, Belfast distributors had lost almost all their trade with the rest of the country. Ultimately, 1920 had been a bad year for the crown in Ireland.[61]

6

SHEEP, SINN FÉINERS AND SOLDIERS

One of the biggest obstacles to republican activity in County Kildare was the large military presence in the county, which dated back to the eighteenth century, giving it deep roots in the community with many financial and emotional ties. Although in 1920 the number of British troops in the county stood at about 6,000, many soldiers had families with them, which provided a sizeable source of revenue in the mid-Kildare area. Such a large military presence had obvious beneficial effects on the economy of the county. Employment was provided for many local men as civilian labourers in the various military barracks. Horses were bred locally and sold to the army. Local contracts for the soldiers' foodstuffs and forage for the horses also made the fortune of many people in the area.[1]

Newbridge, in particular, had benefited from the military presence. The building of the cavalry barracks in 1819 had seen the town of Newbridge rapidly spring up around the huge complex, which held 700 men and up to 1,000 horses. The construction of the barracks took several years and the resulting demand for labour brought many workers to the town, inflating the population. The local landlord, Thomas Eyre Powell, who had provided much of the site for the barracks, realising the potential for trade with the military, built a row of houses, which became shops with living accommodation. This was the foundation of the town, which grew rapidly from a population of 600 inhabitants in 1837 to 3,400 in 1901.[2]

While Naas was an important military centre, the town was also the main urban focal point in the county and did not become as dependent on the army as Newbridge. Over the years there were many incidents between locals and the military – the regular troops were generally popular in the town, but the militia did not have such a good standing.[3] In 1873 the barracks became the depot of the Royal Dublin Fusiliers and drew recruits from the region comprising Dublin, Kildare, Carlow and Wicklow. So began nearly forty years of association between the Dublin Fusiliers and Naas. Several hundred local men joined the British Army during the Great War.

The artillery barracks in Kildare town, completed in 1901, brought about the first increase in the town's population since the Great Famine, but it did not develop great dependence on the military population either, due to its role as a market town and commercial centre for the expanding horse industry in the area.[4]

Hundreds of civilians and soldiers were employed in the building of the Curragh Camp in 1855 and many civilians found employment in barrack workshops, canteens and general maintenance. The camp evolved into the largest military station in Ireland and one of the best equipped training grounds in the

British Isles. It was one of the few examples of the complete permanent military town, entirely self-contained and designed to accommodate a military and civilian population of 10,000. The building of the camp would not only alter forever the landscape of the plain, its environment and its use, but also caused major changes in the lives of the local population.

The neighbouring civilian population had traditionally pastured sheep on the grassy plains of the Curragh for centuries. Now they had to contend with their livestock being killed or injured if they strayed near the army rifle ranges. The Curragh Act of 1870 established that local inhabitants should be allowed pasturage on the Curragh for sheep only, but that no compensation should be paid for injuries claimed as a result of sheep grazing near the camp or rifle ranges and that locals must restrict their presence on the Curragh itself to the designated roads established by the army. Private lands were requisitioned for military manoeuvres, though owners were always compensated for any damage done. While the British thought they were acting fairly in allowing civilians to continue their grazing privileges on the Curragh, the locals resented the fact that their sheep, which had always been there, were now threatened by the hazards of a foreign army.[5]

While there were negative aspects to having the army in Kildare, there was also the positive social aspect of the presence of the military, their families and the many civilians employed by them. The financial benefits generated by the army brought much-needed revenue to all classes of Kildare people. The country gentry welcomed the officers to the seasonal balls, hunting fields, racecourses, polo grounds, cricket pitches and shooting parties throughout the county. Non-commissioned officers and men brought spending power to the shops and hostelries of the neighbouring towns. A major source of entertainment for the civilians of all classes were the military revues, field days, manoeuvres or ceremonial celebrations.

The economic and social bonds which had been cemented between the military and civilian population proved difficult for the republican movement to break down. Thousands of local men had served in the British forces during the Great War and 567 had been killed in action, or died of disease or sickness. The military was, therefore, not a colonial army of strangers – many were married locally – and their presence provided much of the county with its livelihood.[6]

James and Frances Price, both natives of Leitrim, came to New-bridge from Dublin in 1895 and bought a large retail premises, with living accommodation above and a stores yard. They had ten children. Bill, born in Newbridge, in 1904, recalled:

> Newbridge was a grand busy little town when the British Army was here. One lived off the army; no matter what one had to sell the army bought it – from a horse to a chicken. One could poach a couple of salmon or shoot pheasant, anything, the army would buy it – hay, straw, logs. There was no fear in the town or never any violence, except an occasional brawl from over-drinking. But there was no sectarianism; they were part of society and they were welcome.[7]

Kildare had one of Ireland's largest Protestant populations at the time of the War of Independence. The population of County Kildare in 1911 was 66,627 and the census recorded 54,684 Catholics and 11,943 Protestants in the county. Of the Protestant population recorded, there were 10,498 Church of Ireland or Anglicans, 611 Presbyterians and 834 others in the county.[8] Kildare was home to many large and influential landowning families such as the Fitzgeralds at Carton and the Earl of Mayo at Palmerstown. Lord Mayo was one of the most prominent southern loyalists. These loyal families employed butlers, gardeners and staff who were all pro-British. The urban areas all had large numbers of ex-servicemen who were more loyal to the government than they were to the republican movement.

There was a great deal of social interaction between the military and the civilian population. For the officers of the British Army one of the great attractions of service in Kildare was the prospect of hunting with the county and the neighbouring packs of hounds, and of participating in, or attending, the race meetings on the Curragh and at Punchestown, as well as the regimental and other point-to-point fixtures. The Kildare Hunt Club was the principal sporting outlet for the officers from the Curragh, Newbridge, Kildare and Naas Barracks. Membership of the hunt included regular officers living in rented houses locally, who might have individual membership, or gentlemen who hunted on mess subscription from their regiment. The general officer commanding in Ireland and the general officers from the Curragh or Newbridge were usually members.[9]

However, from the beginning of 1919 times were to change. In January of that year the Kildare master of foxhounds received a letter from the secretary of the Naas Sinn Féin club informing him that he would not be permitted to hunt until the prisoners interned in the 'German Plot' were released. Michael O'Kelly reasoned:

In 1919 the repressive policy of the British Government was in full swing against Sinn Féin and raids, arrests and courts martial were taking place all over the country. In retaliation for the association of the ascendency class with this repressive policy, the stoppage of hunt meets was decided upon in several parts of the country. The Naas Sinn Féin Club adopted this policy in order to make a demonstration that might have a salutary effort in bringing home to this class in the county that they could not indulge their hostility to Irish ideals in this way with impunity. It was, therefore, decided that a number of the members should proceed to Betaghstown, Clane, on the occasion of a Hunt Meet there, and with the aid of others from adjoining districts prevent, as far as possible, the Hunt from taking place there. A number volunteered for this purpose and, on the 8th February, they proceeded to the scene of action. Mr. Tommy Harris, with the local men, met those from Naas and a cordon was formed across one of the cross roads by which the Hunt would have to pass on the way to the covert. Those forming the cordon were armed with sticks torn from trees. Individual members of the Hunt on seeing these preparations to make trouble came and expostulated with the obstructors declaring that the Hunt or its members had nothing to do with political affairs. The spokesmen of the obstructors replied that Irishmen had been arrested and sent to English jails for political reasons and that until these were released all hunting would be prevented. They added that certain followers of the Hunt were notoriously hostile to Irish freedom and, on the County Grand Juries, had identified themselves with resolutions passed by them urging the Government to suppress national organisations. Mr. Kerry Supple, County Inspector R.I.C., who was present with some policemen, warned the obstructors of the consequences that might attend interference with the Hunt. The obstructors refused to abandon their position and the followers of the Hunt, seeing that they were determined to persist in their opposition, a conference was held with the Master of the Hunt and as a result the ruse was adopted of taking the obstructors by surprise in changing the draw to another covert to which a different road to that held by the obstructors led. The huntsmen in charge of the hounds, followed by the rest of the Hunt, suddenly made a dash for the road that led to Mount Armstrong and galloped off before further opposition could be offered. The obstructing party had, therefore, to be content with the demonstration such as it was, but it had its effect amongst members of the Hunt and at the same time encouraged active opposition of a like kind in other centres.[10]

According to a *Kildare Observer* report, three dozen Sinn Féiners assembled at Betaghstown to give effect to the decree communicated by the Sinn Féin County Executive to the Master of Fox Hounds and the Secretary of the Kildare Hunt Club, which stated that no hunting would be permitted until untried political prisoners were released. The hunt meet was an exceptionally large one and was confronted by protesters three-deep across the road leading to the first covert to be drawn. County Inspector Supple appealed to Tom Harris and Michael O'Kelly to use their good influence in having the protesters withdraw. After considerable discussion the huntsmen abandoned the first covert and proceeded to Mount Armstrong, some miles away. In the afternoon, the *Observer* said, 'sections of Sinn Féiners were seen patrolling and drilling at the crossroads'.[11]

On 5 March, following advertisements to farmers to attend a protest in favour of the continuance of hunting and racing in Kildare, a large public meeting was held in the courtroom of the

County Courthouse, Naas. There were between 400 and 500 farmers present, chiefly from north Kildare, as farmers from the southern end of the county expressed their inability to attend owing to the meeting clashing with the Athy fair. It was reported as being 'by far the largest and most representative gathering of farmers ever assembled at a meeting in the county'. While the farmers were gathering for the meeting, republicans distributed a leaflet headed 'Fox-hunting or Freedom'.

In explaining that the purpose of the meeting was to protest against organised opposition to hunt meets, the chairman, Joseph O'Connor (Mylerstown), pointed out the gravity, from the farmers' point of view, of interference with fox hunting, stating that the prosperity of the farming community depended to a large extent on the existence of this sport. Large quantities of oats and forage were purchased from the farmers every year by the followers of the hunt. A loss of business to horse breeders, to farming in general, and to local traders was feared, as *The Kildare Observer* said, 'There is perhaps no county in Ireland in which horse-breeding for hunting and sporting measures has become so much a part of the lives of even the smallest farmers as in County Kildare.' A list of 1,532 signatures of landowners was displayed, all asking that hunting and racing should be continued and stating that the Kildare hounds were always welcome to go over their lands. In the audience were several republicans, who said there was no organised canvas of those who were opposed to hunting and that the only means they had of bringing the 'coercionists and anti-Irish elements to book for their hostile displays' was the stopping of the hunt. The culmination of the meeting was that the farmers were prepared to request in writing that the prisoners should be released, but members of the Hunt Club, who were assembled in another room, said that they would not make such a plea as it was a political matter.[12]

While the core issue of the Sinn Féin campaign was its call to have republican political prisoners released, the magistrates and officials who hunted with the Kildare hounds were seen as part of the system which interned republicans and kept them in jail. Another factor that aroused the ire of nationalists was that Gaelic football and hurling matches were closely policed by the RIC – and indeed the organisers of Gaelic games had to apply for permits to the resident magistrates, who were invariably hunt members or supporters. No such restrictions applied to the hunting classes, as a correspondent to *The Kildare Observer*, Gerard Broe of Tipperstown, Straffan, remarked:

> … the supporters of athletics and football were forced by the Government to apply to a magistrate (a Hunt Club member) for a permit before advertising a fixture. This, I suppose, was not political, although the law was administered by a prominent Hunt Club member. As a keen supporter of all branches of sport I would like equal rights also.[13]

The members of the hunt, however, were not in a conciliatory mood. At a subsequent meeting of the Kildare Hounds, a crowd of demonstrators surrounded the hunt members and, according to Lieutenant-Colonel St Leger Moore (Killashee), the hounds were beaten, the horses struck, the riders, including a reverend gentleman, were assaulted and pelted with stones, and a revolver was discharged. He added that the windows of the home of the master of foxhounds had been broken, and warned that if politics invaded sport that not only hunting but also racing, cricket and football would be affected.[14]

In retaliation to the stopping of the hunt in Kildare and other counties, the Hunt Club issued an ultimatum that if its sport across the Kildare countryside was to be blocked then it would pull the national hunt meeting scheduled for Punchestown on 28–29 April 1919. The Hunt Club made the case that the daily hunt meets were necessary to generate the kind of income needed to stage the race meeting. If these were obstructed the Punchestown race meeting would suffer too. In the view of the Hunt committee, 'hunting, Hunt race meetings, and Hunt horse shows stand or fall together'. A week later a letter writer to *The Kildare Observer*, signing his name 'Tomás', criticised the small and exclusive body who sought to control racing, 'the sport of all classes', and told St Leger Moore to 'wait and see, Colonel, we are only at the beginning of the road, not the end as you seem to think'. The omens were not good when word came through that the National Hunt Committee had cancelled the Fairyhouse meeting on Easter Monday as retaliation for the Sinn Féin campaign of stopping the country hunt meetings. The Kildare Hunt followed suit and the Punchestown meeting was duly abandoned. The newspapers lamented the loss of business not only in the county, but in Dublin, too. Hotels and boarding houses were quiet and there was none of the traditional decorating of houses in the Naas district. With the loss of thousands of pounds in the economic coffers, the business people of the county were forcefully made aware that the boom days of the war were gone and a different world was being created.[15]

Hunting was abandoned for the season and attitudes towards the hunt hardened considerably. Athy UDC passed a resolution that 'in the present circumstances of the county' no further hunting should be allowed to take place 'in which the military or upholders of British law are allowed to participate' and called on all farmers to prevent the hunt crossing their lands.

Punchestown was again abandoned in 1920. The meeting was held in 1921, however, and it was judged to have been particularly successful, though there was an unpleasant incident when two armed men held up the driver and stole the Lord Lieutenant's Crossley saloon.[16]

The country gentry also lost another of their favoured pastimes, as shooting was virtually impossible since all guns and cartridges had to be surrendered to the military. As the country became increasingly violent, the nocturnal knockings on country-house doors grew ever more frequent; there were no attacks on Protestants in Kildare, but the IRA carried out widespread raids on the houses of the gentry in search of arms. However, Kildare got off lightly. No big houses were burned, making it one of only six counties in which this was the case. Raids for arms were more frequent, however. The men who raided Carton House were polite to the butler and avoided waking the young Duke's uncle, Lord Frederick Fitzgerald, but they took, among other things, the revolver of Lieutenant Desmond Fitzgerald (killed in action in 1916), which had been sent back from France.[17]

There were violent attacks on some landowners and houses, but few were recorded in Kildare. At Ballindoolin on 12 August 1920 William Tyrell was aroused at midnight by a loud knocking on his hall door. He stuck his head out the window, and, on seeing a number of men, armed himself with a revolver and fired a number of shots at them. He believed he saw one man fall and thought he might have wounded a second. The men picked up their wounded comrade and took cover in the shrubbery in front of the house. Tyrell claimed they fired at least thirty shots at the house before disbanding. The Palmerstown home of Lord Mayo – one of the leading southern unionists – was also visited that month and a lodge house damaged.[18]

As Edward 'Cub' Kennedy of Bishopscourt, Kill, was driving through the streets of Dublin with a friend alongside him and his two schoolboy sons in the back, their car was fired upon. As they drove on, unscathed except for a broken windscreen, the friend observed wryly, 'That was worse than a grouse drive.'[19]

Other IRA activities, such as the trenching of roads and blowing up of bridges, were more a nuisance than anything else. Mary Findlater, daughter of Henry de Courcy Wheeler, lived at Robertstown House and recalled:

During the troubles of the 1920s when my father was out and about he brought with him a spade and two planks, to get across trenches dug across the road, and a saw to cut through branches where trees had been felled. We sometimes had to climb over two or three trees getting from our house in Robertstown to the church in Kilmeague. On yet another occasion, when the family were having breakfast in Robertstown House, a platoon of British soldiers suddenly rushed into the house, tore around the house, and tore out again. They were looking for a fugitive, and a few minutes later a little officer came panting in and asked had we seen his platoon. He had lost it.[20]

As the terror continued, many landlords left the country due to attacks on their family homes. The social scene, however, improved slightly in 1921. While, the Dublin Spring Show had to be abandoned owing to a coal strike, Punchestown was particularly successful and there was racing also at Leopardstown and at the Curragh. The social importance of Punchestown was obvious, with guest parties from every 'big house' in the county, including Palmerstown, Gowran Grange, Killashee, Kinneagh and Courtown.

On 27 April 1921, the Catholic Viscount FitzAlan replaced Lord French as Viceroy. For the first time since the reign of James II, the sovereign's representative attended Mass in Dublin; but what was more important was that FitzAlan seemed to come as an emissary of peace. (His appointment was possible because Section 37 of the Government of Ireland Act 1920 had been brought into force shortly beforehand. That provision provided that no British subject would be disqualified from holding the position on account of his religious belief.) Concerning the announcement of his impending appointment, the *Daily Chronicle* observed that 'the conciliatory motive of his appointment [being a Roman Catholic] is obvious … it is an olive branch in place of a dictatorship'. After he had been in Ireland a month, FitzAlan publicly admitted that the Black and Tans had committed 'crimes, horrible crimes'. The omens for peace finally looked good.[21]

7

NO ORDINARY WOMEN: CUMANN NA MBAN IN KILDARE

Cumann na mBan emerged in 1914, at a time when society did not encourage the participation of women in politics. The movement had its origins in two powerful forces that were driving rapid political and social transitions in Ireland in the first decades of the twentieth century: feminism and nationalism.[1]

Present at the inaugural meeting of the Irish Volunteers in November 1913 were many nationalistic-minded women who were told by the organisers of the Volunteers that there was a role for the women of Ireland to play in the coming struggle. Some of these women were not content with working in a subsidiary capacity for the Volunteers and the idea of a separate women's organisation quickly gathered momentum. After a series of informal meetings, the inaugural public meeting of Cumann na mBan took place in Wynn's Hotel, Dublin, on 2 April 1914.[2] It was a smaller event than the Volunteers' inaugural meeting, with, according to *The Irish Times*, 'about 100 ladies present'.[3] Feminists such as Hannah Sheehy-Skeffington poured scorn on the new organisation because it was merely an auxiliary to the all-male Volunteers. However, it is suggested by some that the attendees were generally more committed to Irish separatism than their male counterparts in the Volunteers. Cal McCarthy, in *Cumann na mBan and the Irish Revolution*, wrote:

> This was a small but determined group of women with an intense desire for Irish self-determination. Unlike the men who flocked to the ranks of the Volunteers, this women's group would not provide much adventure, excitement or glamour for its members. Indeed, from the minute attendance it must have been evident that their activities would not meet with the same support as those of their male counterparts. Yet their resolve to assist in securing Irish self-rule would not allow them to be deterred. It is little wonder then, that Cumann na mBan were to become one of the most uncompromisingly nationalist (and later republican) groups.[4]

Membership of the new organisation was to be confined to women of Irish birth or descent, and the name Cumann na mBan literally translates as 'council of women', though the organisation itself tended to translate it as 'Irishwomen's Council'. Its first constitution declared the organisation's aims as:

> To advance the cause of Irish liberty.
> To organise Irishwomen in the furtherance of this object.
> To assist in arming and equipping a body of Irishmen for the defence of Ireland.
> To form a fund for these purposes to be called the 'Defence of Ireland Fund.'

In addition to assisting in equipping and arming the Volunteers, branches were expected to 'keep in touch with their local Volunteer battalions, appear at the parades, and identify themselves with Volunteer work in every suitable way'.[5] However, the organisation of Cumann na mBan branches throughout the country was initially slow, as Irishwomen did not seem too enamoured with the new organisation.[6]

On 27 August 1914 a branch was formed in Newbridge, County Kildare. At the Town Hall a local committee, which was 'large and representative', was formed from 'the women of Newbridge and districts adjoining'. On the motion of the Rev. Father Phelan, CC, the chair was taken by Mr P. J. Doyle, JP. The meeting was addressed by Miss Elizabeth Bloxham, one of the founding members of Cumann na mBan. Miss Bloxham told the meeting that Cumann na mBan urged 'all Irishwomen to become members of the organisation, and in the course of instruction will be included First Aid and ambulance classes, while arrangements will be made for contributions to the general equipment fund'. Mr Doyle, in his address, said that Miss Bloxham had earlier organised the Cumann na mBan branches in Naas, Kildare and Athy, and 'looked on the Co. Kildare almost as her special charge'. Miss Bloxham said, 'there was now no county as organised as the Co. Kildare'. She stated that the women of Ireland should help equip their husbands, sons or relatives. The home attitude always stimulated and she hoped Irishwomen would help their men in the cause:

In such movements woman was practically as strong as man. The Cumann na mBan was one with the Irish Volunteers. They drill, we don't, but if the necessity arose there is nothing that ever could be done by women in any country that we Irish women cannot do.[7]

Elizabeth Bloxham was a young Anglican from the west of Ireland. Because of her experience as a public speaker at literary and suffragette meetings, she was appointed as a national organiser for Cumann na mBan. She was also a teacher from a farming background who spent her school holidays travelling around Ireland forming branches of the movement.[8] These meetings were a joint venture between the Volunteers and Cumann na mBan. Each branch of Cumann na mBan was set up in association with a branch of the Irish Volunteers. They were separate organisations, but always worked together. To set up a branch of Cumann na mBan required a minimum of fifteen women.[9]

Another organiser for Cumann na mBan in County Kildare, Brigid O'Mullane from Sligo, outlined the procedure for organising branches of the movement:

It was my custom to contact the Volunteer O/C, who gave me the names of reliable girls. Having got the names, I convened a meeting generally at the private house of one of the girls; occasionally it might be at a local hall or even a barn. I first lectured the girls on the aims and objects of the organisation, and the work they would be asked to do. I had a good deal of prejudice to overcome on the part of the parents, who did not mind their boys taking part in a military movement, but who had never heard of, and were reluctant to accept, the idea of a body of gun-women. It was, of course a rather startling innovation and, in that way, Cumann na mBan can claim to have been the pioneers in establishing what was undoubtedly a women's auxiliary of an army. I fully understood this attitude and eventually, in most cases, succeeded in overcoming this prejudice.

At the inauguration meeting of each branch, having lectured the girls, I got them to elect a President, Captain, Honorary Secretary and Treasurer and committee members. I advised them to meet, if possible, weekly. Before I left them, I always tried to get the local doctor or nurse to give the branch a course of first-aid lectures, and an I.R.A. officer to instruct them in drill, signalling, dispatch-carrying, cleaning and unloading arms. Each branch paid an affiliation fee of ten shillings to Headquarters and thus became entitled to send a representative to the annual convention at Headquarters. The branches then were in close contact with General Headquarters. While preserving their separate identity, the branches worked in close conjunction with the local I.R.A. companies, which constantly availed of their services in activities, such as the carrying of arms and ammunition, dispatch carrying, intelligence work, getting safe houses for wanted men, looking after the wounded, when necessary, seeing to the wants of prisoners, and collecting funds for the Volunteers. For the latter purpose, they organised concerts, céilidhthe, aeridheachta.[10]

Brigid O'Mullane was very lucky to survive two harrowing experiences while reorganising the local Cumann na mBan branch in Naas. She arrived in November 1920 at the same time as local IRA commandant, Tom Harris, was arrested, and was fired on by the raiding Black and Tans, but escaped. Another of her contacts, Paddy Moran, was also arrested and the presence of a 'suspicious' person in the area, i.e. Brigid O'Mullane, led local Volunteers to believe she was a British spy. They made plans to assassinate her. Luckily, the intelligence officer for the area confirmed her identity and the danger was averted.[11]

John Redmond had formed a group in September 1914 – The Irish Volunteer Aid Association – to do precisely the same work for the National Volunteers as Cumann na mBan had undertaken. This would be staffed and governed by men; women could join and work for it, but no woman had been appointed to its committee. There were many respectable citizens who wanted to help, but whose loyalty was assumed to be to the crown and so could not be recruited into the republican movement. They joined this organisation, but it never had the same prominence or effectiveness as Cumann na mBan and eventually died out.[12]

In September 1914, when the Irish Volunteers split, Cumann na mBan tried to remain neutral and, initially, no support for either side was publicly announced. However, on 6 October 1914, after a specially convened meeting, it was declared that: 'As the Women's section of the Irish Volunteers we wish at this time to remind our members that they should abide loyally by the constitution of our Organisation'.[13]

A convention was called in November 1914 at which a vote on whether to support John Redmond was lost by eighty-eight votes to twenty-eight. Several members at the meeting resigned, leading to a split in Cumann na mBan. While some branches declared for the National Volunteers, the rump of the organisation declared allegiance to the Irish Volunteers. They reformed as the (second) Cumann na mBan, which was committed solely to the ideals of separatist nationalism. Declarations of support for the Redmond faction were made through the pages of the *National Volunteer* by the Naas and Athy branches. Cumann na mBan lost more than half its membership nationally during the split.[14]

After the division Cumann na mBan took on a much more militaristic bearing and by the beginning of 1916 had become a small but reasonably well-organised and partially trained, quasi-military organisation.[15] Due to Eoin MacNeill's countermanding order only two branches mobilised in Dublin on Easter Monday, but as soon as hostilities began, individual Cumann na mBan members began to make their way to the Dublin city garrisons. These women, individually, or in little groups, had to depend on their own initiative in order to make their contribution to the fight. Eventually, there were over thirty women in the GPO garrison, though not all were Cumann na mBan members.[16] The women of 1916 carried dispatches, tended the wounded, cooked and distributed food. Among the Dublin garrisons there was at least one woman from County Kildare – Mrs D. Beatty, née Daly, from Kildare town.[17]

The re-forming of Cumann na mBan after the 1916 Rising was a priority. Countess Markievicz, a veteran of Easter Week, became involved with the movement then and was elected president at the 1917 convention. At Bodenstown in 1917, at the annual commemoration to Wolfe Tone, she addressed the crowd. The commemoration was a markedly Sinn Féin affair, a party way ahead of its time in its treatment of women. From its formation Sinn Féin had made it clear that its ideology welcomed women members on the same basis as men.[18] Markievicz ended her address by asking the crowd to 'never cease in their efforts until Ireland was a Nation and when the time came to acknowledge the work performed by her and her sex, they would concede them those rights and privileges to which they had claim'.[19]

The conscription crisis in July 1918 led Cumann na mBan into a new phase of militant activity. They participated in the campaign by holding anti-conscription meetings, distributing leaflets, painting walls and advising on and signing the anti-conscription pledge. Women also played a major role in the general election of 1918, canvassing and propagandising for Sinn Féin. Constance Markievicz became the first woman to be elected to Westminster, though she did not take her seat.[20]

While thousands of women believed as fervently and participated as enthusiastically as male republicans – either as members of Cumann na mBan, the Irish Citizen Army, Sinn Féin, or as individuals outside any formal body – they would not be called upon to take up arms. Nevertheless, as the revolution gathered force, so too did the roles of women within the national movement.

Under the auspices of Cumann na mBan republican women continued to take on traditional female roles in the War of Independence, serving as nurses, messengers, cooks and proprietors of safe houses. Mollie Curran, Dunshane, Kilcullen, was fifteen when the Black and Tans arrived in Naas in March 1920:

> My brother Stephen was over the IRA unit in Two Mile House and he used to train the lads over there. We formed a small unit of Cumann na mBan and we used to do drilling and exercises out in the field. We used to go out on camps to the Ballymore-Eustace area and we learned Morse code in the hall in Two Mile House.

Mollie had a more direct involvement in the military campaign when information she supplied to Naas officer Jimmy Whyte led to an ambush on a lorry of Black and Tans near Harristown. 'The Naas lads threw some sort of bomb at the lorry, but I don't think there was anybody injured'.[21]

Beyond these traditional roles, however, women started to appear on political platforms in greater numbers, culminating with their participation in the Dáil during the Treaty debates.[22] During the War of Independence and the Civil War, Cumann na mBan provided uniformed guards of honour at republican funerals. In part this was expediency. For obvious reasons it was risky for known IRA men to appear at public funerals. For example, when Kill Company marched behind Volunteer Seán O'Sullivan's coffin in Naas in May 1921, seven of them were arrested.[23]

During the War of Independence the RIC never attempted to tabulate statistics for Cumann na mBan in several counties, among them Kildare, so there are no figures for membership of the organisation in the county.[24] What is known is that in 1921 there were at least ten Cumann na mBan branches in Kildare – Athy, Naas, Newbridge, Kildare town, Kill, Two-Mile-House, Celbridge, Maynooth, Leixlip and Kilcock – with varying degrees of membership. Most branches had only a few members and relied on the mothers, sisters and wives of active republicans. Jim Dunne, Kill, described the local scene in 1922:

> ... all our dispatches went through the Misses Barnewall and Misses B. and Fanny O'Connor, Elm Hall, Celbridge. Misses May and Fanny Dunne, my sisters at Kill, and Miss Grehan, Naas, handled our despatches and carried arms, etc., for our men. Miss Peg Daly was the principal Cumann na mBan girl in Kildare Town.[25]

Brigid and Fanny O'Connor were sisters of Kildare TD Art

O'Connor; May and Fanny Dunne were sisters of Jim Dunne, whose father was Captain Pat Dunne, Kill Company.

The 1921 Cumann na mBan convention reported a figure of 702 Irish branches, with a membership of between 11,000 and 12,000 members.[26] Forty republican women were in prison at the time of the Truce (11 July 1921).[27] However, none were from Kildare, though by the end of the Civil War five Kildare women were incarcerated.[28]

By the time the Truce was declared, Cumann na mBan had reached the pinnacle of its success. The movement had provided immeasurable assistance to the IRA in the war with the crown forces. At the annual convention held in Dublin in October 1921, Countess Markievicz, in her presidential address, observed:

What has been won has been won by the fighting men and women of Ireland and no one else ... the men in the country tell me they never could have carried on without the help of Cumann na mBan.[29]

8

THE INTELLIGENCE WAR

The most important battle of the War of Independence was the struggle for superiority in the area of 'Intelligence', and the key contribution made by Kildare Volunteers to the war was in this area. Many of the IRA intelligence officers worked in British institutions and supplied their colleagues with top-secret details. The most important of these double agents was Eamon Broy, a native of County Kildare, who served as a typist in the detective office of the DMP. He allowed Michael Collins access to the headquarters of the Dublin detective force in Brunswick (now Pearse) Street in April 1919.

Eamon (Ned) Broy was born on 22 December 1887 in Ballinure, Rathangan, the son of Patrick Broy, farmer, and his wife, Mary (née Barry). An ancestor, John Broy, had fought with the rebels in 1798 and a hedge school had been held on the Broy farmland during the Penal Law days. Broy was educated locally, where memories of British atrocities during 1798 were still vivid.[1] He joined the RIC on 2 August 1910 and the DMP on 20 January 1911. In 1915 Broy moved from the uniformed to the detective branch and was ultimately assigned to the headquarters of G Division as a confidential clerk.

Broy was not an ardent supporter of the ruling regime and initially joined the DMP for its good athletic facilities and its reputation for being less political and more liberal than the RIC. When he joined G Division Broy believed that Home Rule was imminent. However, the Easter Rising and its aftermath led him to the realisation that independence would, in all likelihood, only come through force. In March 1917 Broy decided to assist the Volunteers. He initially made contact with the republican movement through Harry O'Hanrachain, a member of the IRB and later a courier in Collins' intelligence network.[2] Broy recalled:

> There was strong feeling amongst the Irish people that all their risings such as those in 1642, 1798, 1867 and 1883 had been defeated by informers. It was one of the aims of the I.R.A. at a later date, with whom I had the honour of co-operating, to remove such a source of danger to the movement and which necessitated the use of such violent methods.[3]

Broy established his credibility by warning about the imminent arrest of two middle-ranking members of Sinn Féin, and shortly afterwards began to pass on confidential documents and police codes. In March 1918, with the threat of conscription, the Irish Volunteers established a General Headquarters staff to organise effective resistance. Collins was officially appointed director of organisation, but he had already started to establish a small group of spies within Dublin Castle. Broy had not yet met Collins and was unaware of the other agents, but he became central to the intelligence network then being constructed. This became apparent in May 1918, when the Castle authorities prepared to arrest republicans in the 'German Plot'. On 17 May Broy handed a list of names of those to be arrested that night to O'Hanrachain, who passed it to Collins. Although Collins issued a warning, many, such as de Valera, chose to remain where they were and be arrested to highlight the injustices of the governing regime. Despite this, the incident cemented Collins as the *de facto* head of intelligence and in turn showed him that Broy would be central to the success of his intelligence war.[4]

Collins, like Broy, understood precisely where the police fitted into the British system. By this time Broy had been a policeman for eight years and brought Collins inside information on how the system worked and how the men were trained, thought and felt. The DMP was divided into six divisions, A to F, plus G, the political division, which investigated anyone who was thought to be disloyal to the British authorities. As a clerk, Broy was not of high rank, but he had access to the most confidential files of the government intelligence services operating within Ireland. Each G man had his own notebook and every night its contents were transferred to a large central book in the headquarters of G Division in Brunswick Street. Daily and weekly reports were made to the government. Broy claimed 'that about ninety per cent of R.I.C. information reached the G Division (and was transmitted by me to the Irish Volunteers from March, 1917, when I got charge of it, until 1921)'.[5]

Over the following years Broy's provision of information proved vital to the efforts of the republican movement generally and Collins specifically. Collins' desire to keep his contacts shrouded in secrecy meant that he and Broy did not meet until April 1919, when Broy smuggled him into G Division head-quarters at Brunswick Street, enabling him to trawl through secret files for eight hours. Encountering an old comrade, Seán Nunan, on his way there, Collins brought him along for the 'craic'. Broy, Collins and Nunan remained there from 11 p.m. until 7 a.m. A nervous Broy stood guard as Collins methodically worked through the files as if he were a police employee. When he came across his own file, Collins briefly scanned it before putting it in his briefcase. In Brunswick Street Collins had the entire police intelligence system before him. He saw what he was up against and how to combat the enemy.[6]

Two days later Collins began his intelligence war in earnest when he distributed lists of junior detectives (gathered from his night in Brunswick Street) to the Dublin Brigade. In most cases the detectives were followed and taken down alleyways, where various methods of persuasion were used to dissuade them from working against Collins. The policy of shooting detectives began in July 1919, when Broy named Patrick Smyth, a detective sergeant in G Division, as dangerous. Towards the end of 1919 a letter written by Henry Quinlisk, an ex-British soldier and former member of Casement's Irish Brigade, to the Under Secretary, was copied by Broy and passed on to Collins. Quinlisk was working as a double agent for the British. Collins sent him off to Cork on a wild goose chase, where the Cork IRA were waiting for him. His body was later found in a ditch.

Collins himself had several near brushes with the crown forces, but Broy was able to forewarn him. In an effort to halt the killings of prominent G men, the British brought in Detective Inspector

F. Redmond from Belfast. Redmond informed Detective David Neligan that he had arranged a meeting with Collins. Neligan was also working for Collins and passed the information on to Broy who quickly contacted Collins. A couple of days later the Squad ambushed Redmond. He was wearing a bulletproof vest, but the Squad knew this, so they shot him in the head.[7]

The hunt for Collins went on; the British hoped to pick him up at the April Dáil sittings, but with Broy's help he again escaped. Another night Collins was with Broy and his other 'Castle Spies', David Neligan and James MacNamara, when their car was stopped at a checkpoint. Collins got out of the car, flashed a phoney detective pass and commiserated with the officer in charge on 'these dreadful ambushes'. Broy called, 'Step in, Sergeant', and 'Sergeant' Collins bid the officer goodnight and hopped back into the car, bearing documents that would have put all four in jeopardy.[8]

Neligan was an important Castle Spy. On first meeting Broy, Neligan suspected that he was no friend 'of the regime'. He described him:

> Broy was about twenty-six, broad-faced, rather stooped, an enigmatic character. A native of Kildare, he had only one love, athletics, and one hate, the British Empire. As he was an official typist, he made an extra carbon copy of every confidential report for Collins. Collins stored up these – and when they were found – stored up trouble for Broy.[9]

Although he was genuinely committed to the republican movement and enjoyed the power it gave him, Broy was plagued by his conflicting loyalties to his job on one hand and his country on the other. He obtained promotion to pay sergeant in the detective's superintendent's office before being arrested in March 1921 following the discovery of documents typed by him in the flat of republican sympathiser Eileen McGrane. An armoured car called at the Brunswick Street office while Broy was having his tea. Two British officers came in, arrested him and brought him to Arbour Hill Military Prison. It was rumoured that he was to be executed. Collins planned to rescue him, but Neligan came up with another plan. Broy's superior superintendent was threatened by Collins and, desiring a healthy life, burned Broy's papers, leaving no evidence to convict him. Broy pleaded another was responsible for his own activities, naming a detective who shared his office and who had recently left for England. This was arranged by Collins through inducement and threat. After the Truce Collins saw to it that this man was sent a return ticket to Ireland. Collins then wrote and signed a letter, which he sent into the Castle, arranging for it to be discovered. The letter asked what all the fuss about Broy was, for this man had always been an enemy of the republican movement. Still under suspicion, Broy was held in custody until after the Truce. Following his release he travelled to London with the Treaty delegation as Collins' private secretary and bodyguard.[10]

It is obvious from his witness statement that Broy had great affection for Collins, for whom he would have laid down his life. Collins inspired a great loyalty from all who met him and Broy was no different. When he boasted about having been paid by the British government for the time he spent in prison, Collins asked to see the money, which he promptly seized and announced that Broy would have to 'wrastle' him for it. Broy said:

So we set to and I won, but I don't believe he did his best. That was one of his tricks to let the other man win. I still do not know whether I would have been able to beat him in an out-and-out wrestling match. In any case none of us would use full force against him, even in play, as to us all he was a sacred personage, the very embodiment and personification of Irish resistance.[11]

As Kildare was in the direct line of communication between the west and south of Ireland and GHQ, their geographical position kept the Kildare Volunteers very busy. Patrick Colgan stated that Volunteers made several journeys to Dublin each day. Colgan appointed Michael Fay (Celbridge), a medical student at University College Dublin (UCD), as courier. Fay sacrificed his university career and refused to accept any payment for his work, despite daily cycling back and forth to Dublin from Celbridge. Sometimes he made three journeys to Dublin and back in a day, bringing information to and from Commandant Colgan in Kildare to GHQ.[12]

All-Ireland footballer Frank 'Joyce' Conlan from Newbridge, who worked as a railway employee, was also an intelligence operative for Collins, providing information on troop movements up and down the country. He became an intelligence officer for Kildare, though very few knew he was actively involved. It was only after the Civil War, when IRA medals were being presented, that many found out the extent of Conlan's involvement.

Another operative was Philip Kennedy from Monread, Naas. He joined the Irish Volunteers in 1915 and became an intelligence officer in Kingstown (Dun Laoghaire) from 1918–21, reporting on troop movements and comings and goings at Ireland's main passenger seaport.[13]

Collins also had important spies in Naas RIC Barracks: Gerry Maher and Patrick Casey. Sergeant Gerry Maher was the confidential clerk to County Inspector Supple at Naas. He passed on details of a new cipher to Collins through a confidant, Seán Kavanagh, the newly appointed Chief Intelligence Officer for County Kildare. Born in Tralee, Kavanagh had worked on behalf of the Gaelic League as an Irish teacher in County Kildare. He learned that Maher passed on information, through Alfie Sweeney, to local Volunteers that their homes were about to be raided. Kavanagh called at Maher's home and told him frankly what he wanted. 'You're the man I've been waiting for for years,' Maher said, explaining that he had tried to get in contact with the republican movement but nobody seemed to be interested. As confidential clerk he had access to the key of the new police code, the circulation of which was restricted to those of county inspector rank. He turned over the key to the code then in use and Collins provided him with wax to make an impression of the actual key that Inspector Supple used to open the safe in his office.

Seán Kavanagh visited Maher's house two or three times a week, always at night, either to collect information or to pass on queries from Collins. A courier system was established which could send written messages to or from Collins through the ticket collector at Sallins railway station within a few hours. The collector passed letters to sympathetic guards on the mainline trains who delivered them to a clerk at Kingsbridge station, who passed them to Collins. The code was changed periodically and a new cipher was passed on to each county inspector. Maher, of course, had access to new ciphers and passed them on to the IRA.

Maher recruited a fellow RIC man, Constable Patrick Casey, who took over Maher's duties whenever the latter was absent on leave or through illness. Towards the end of 1920 the only place where the codes for the RIC, military or naval forces could be had was from Gerry Maher at Naas. Maher continued to pass information and refused promotion in order to do his work. Realising that his activities were arousing suspicion, he resigned at the end of 1920, but was replaced by Paddy Casey, who continued assisting the IRA, again through Kavanagh, until the latter's arrest and imprisonment in Kilmainham Jail in January 1921. James Clancy, Newbridge, replaced Kavanagh as a channel of information.

While the Maher-Kavanagh network operated, Kavanagh was under orders from Collins to have no dealings with the local IRA. The only man who knew officially of the network was Tom Harris, Kildare Battalion OC. Kavanagh's intelligence service also received important information from a member of the clerical staff in the office of the crown solicitor in Naas.[14]

The crown used the country's train system for courier work and to transport mail. Many railway employees were working for the IRA as intelligence operatives on the Kildare railway system. Kavanagh recalled:

I found a very reliable man at Sallins station, James Lennon, the ticket collector, who handed letters from [Seán] O'Connell [a railway clerk at Kingsbridge station] to one of a small number of guards and conductors on main line trains whose names were supplied to me by O'Connell, and also received letters from them to me. This system worked perfectly up to my arrest on 15 January, 1921, and similar systems were, of course, in use on the other railway lines out of Dublin.

Raids for Government mails had not been carried out officially for a considerable time prior to late November, 1920, when Collins asked me to raid the night mail train from Cork occasionally and collect the 'Castle' mailbag from the Post Office sorting van. The train stopped at almost every station and passed through County Kildare between 2 and 3 a.m. I carried out the raids about once a week on average, usually accompanied by one or two trusted local Volunteers and with full co-operation of the Post Office sorting staff, varying our attentions to the different stations of Sallins, Newbridge and Kildare. On the first raid I asked for and was handed No. 3 bag; on each subsequent visit it was handed to me the moment we appeared. Surprisingly the police made no attempt to prevent this activity of which they must have received reports, and it came to an end, as far as I was concerned, only on my arrest.[15]

From March to July 1920 increasing numbers of raids were re-corded by Dublin Castle on post offices in the county. The IRA inspected mail addressed to British forces and which had come from British sources, and relayed any important information to General Headquarters. From the end of July there was a shift from raiding post offices to raiding cars and trains carrying post and also holding up postmen. Raids on mail were particularly important due to the number of military stationed in the county; GHQ needed to obtain as much information as they could on troop movements. Furthermore, because of its geographical loca-tion, all correspondence from Dublin Castle, the centre of British operations in Ireland, for anywhere in the midlands, the west or south, passed through Kildare. By intercepting these letters the IRA gained vital information on all aspects of the crown opera-tions over much of the country.

9

A CALICO SHACK IN KILDARE

The internment of republican prisoners is as old as the Irish republican struggle, and is an aspect of the war in which Kildare played a significant part. The years 1913 to 1923 were the most turbulent in twentieth-century Irish history, with widespread political unrest, extreme violence and momentous constitutional change. Faced with armed insurrection and revolutionary claims to democratic legitimacy, the British government responded with increasingly harsh emergency powers. In late 1920, when the time period for the use of the Defence of the Realm Act (DORA) legislation ran out, internment without trial was introduced, which led to thousands of men and women being imprisoned under emergency law.[1]

The main purpose of internment was to remove an organised and potential threat, but the British government and intelligence system were fighting a war blindfolded. The main difficulty experienced throughout for them was one of identity. Often the British did not know who they were looking for, or even arresting. The aim of internment was to remove potential combatants from the battlefield and if some innocent person was taken away, so be it.

The escalation of conflict in Ireland led, in April 1919, to the strengthening of DORA, with four new key regulations: imposing restrictions on meetings, the keeping of firearms and motor vehicles, and the wearing of uniforms; authorising internment without trial; the operation of courts martial; and the creation of 'Special Military Areas' (SMAs), which could be sealed off and searched by the military.[2] However, the power to issue regulations under DORA was technically only exercisable 'during the continuance of the present war', i.e. the Great War. So, on 9 August 1920, the Restoration of Order in Ireland Act (ROIA) became law, legislating, amongst other things, for the replacement of coroners' courts with military courts of inquiry and for courts martial to impose the death penalty.

The introduction of the ROIA was followed by a general escalation of IRA activities. Orders were given in late 1920 to arrest all leaders of the IRA and other 'wanted men' and 'if sufficient evidence was not available to secure a conviction, to forward their names for internment in Ireland'.[3]

The first use of the Curragh for holding detainees came when seventeen men from County Kildare were arrested during Easter Week 1916 and were confined at Hare Park Camp, the Curragh.[4] Hare Park Camp had initially been built to billet large numbers of troops during the Great War, but was converted for sorting and holding prisoners during the Easter Rising. (The camp took its name because of its location on the edge of the former Kildare Hunt Club, Hare Park site.)[5] During the War of Independence 400 men were held at various times in Hare Park Camp.

The main internment camp for republicans was at Ballykinlar, County Down, but it was soon filled to capacity and other
accommodation was required. Another internment camp was
therefore constructed some 400m north-west of the Gibbet
Rath, on the Curragh of Kildare, to house about 1,500 men.
Known as the Rath Camp, it took its name from the historic
Gibbet Rath – a large, earthen, historic mound – and was close
to the main road from Newbridge to Kildare.[6] On 12 March
1921 the *Leinster Leader* reported, 'Another internment camp,
conducted on the same lines as the Ballykinlar Camp, has been
opened at the Rath, Curragh. A large number of prisoners have
been transferred from the Hare Park Camp to the Rath, where
no visits are allowed'.[7]

The new camp was laid out on the south edge of the Curragh
Camp, directly opposite the racecourse grandstand. It consisted
of about ten acres of the Curragh plain enclosed in a rectangle of
barbed wire entanglements. There were two fences ten feet high,
separated by a passage twenty feet wide, which was patrolled by
sentries. The prisoners called this 'no man's land'. At each corner
of the compound stood high blockhouses from which powerful
searchlights lit up the centre passage. The watchtowers were
manned day and night by sentries armed with rifles and machine
guns, who called out 'All's well', on the stroke of the hour
throughout the night. Beyond the main barrier, the camp was
surrounded by another fence consisting of five single strands of
barbed wire about four feet high. This fence was designed, not to
keep the prisoners in, but rather to prevent animals approaching
the main enclosure. Nevertheless, it was a further obstacle to
the possibility of escape. Additionally, a large searchlight was

mounted on the watchtower of the main military camp. During the hours of darkness its beam lit up the entire Curragh plain.[8]

Inside the enclosure there were some fifty to sixty wooden huts – which served as sleeping quarters for 1,200 to 1,500 men – a hospital, canteen, cook-house, chapel and library. There was a sports ground large enough to provide a football pitch.[9] The huts were wooden and some were bugged, though the practice was not particularly effective. Intelligence staff for the camp were introduced under the guise of censors.[10] A British study of the 1916–21 period known as 'The record of the rebellion' commented:

> Microphones and detectaphones were used to a certain extent. Their value depended on the type of wooden building in which they were situated and they were useless in buildings such as wooden huts where every noise was magnified. Consequently, they were not effective in internment camps, but the prisoners believed they were installed everywhere.

One wire and bug, found behind the bed of the prisoners' camp commandant, led to the British quarters. The prisoners – to their amusement and the guards' embarrassment – used this wire as a clothesline.[11]

The Rath Camp was opened in March 1921 and in early April the first draft of about 100 prisoners arrived from Arbour Hill Jail in Dublin. One of the first prisoners from Kildare was Sylvester Delahunt, from Tuckmill, Straffan, who was arrested in March 1921 and interned there until December. Another internee was R. McDermott from Athy, who was quoted in the *Leinster Leader* as saying: 'Rath Camp is nice, but there's no place like home'. Other internees from the county were Seán Hayden, Athy; Tom Behan, Rathangan; Frank Bourke, Carbury; brothers John and Peter Traynor, Woolpack, Kill; Pat Dunne and Tom Domican, Kill; Matthew Cardiff and Thomas Wilmot, Athgarvan; Art Doran, Ballymore-Eustace; and T. J. Williams and Michael O'Kelly, Naas.[12]

As more men arrived there was a need for organisation and the IRA leadership soon took over these responsibilities. The prisoners organised life within the camp and enforced their own discipline. Tom Byrne, who escaped in a mass breakout in September, wrote:

We ran the camp ourselves, making our own paths out of concrete blocks. In other ways, too, we were allowed within limits to improve our housing conditions. But such concessions were purely domestic and there was no leniency in the manner in which we were guarded for our jailers were constantly on the watch to offset attempts at escape. To try and catch us out there would be sudden swoops on the huts with intensive searches and the barbed wire was being constantly strengthened ... So far only one prisoner had been able to make his getaway from the Rath Camp and he had himself carried out in a laundry basket. Next night the British, not knowing how he got out, tried to scare us by shooting a dummy figure which they had put in the wire.[13]

Life in the camp was dreary and monotonous: the same surroundings, the same dull routine, day after day, week after week. No visits were allowed but morale was kept up by organising concerts, playing football, planning escapes and letter-writing. One of the first escapes took place towards the end of April and was facilitated by some workmen engaged in the completion of the construction of the camp. Their entry and exit was controlled by a pass system and military guards supervised their work. Rory O'Connor managed to talk to two of the workmen and arranged that they would stay away from work on a certain Saturday. Their overalls and passes were brought in by another worker and handed over to O'Connor, who duly walked out of the gate with another prisoner.[14]

The routine of the camp was dictated by two disciplinary systems. On the one hand, the British regulations set the times when the internees were locked up and let out, the number of letters they might write and the amount of food provided. On the other, the internees had their own disciplinary system which dealt with the 'fatigues' allotted to the prisoners. These fatigues were mainly devoted to keeping the huts clean, hygienic and orderly.[15]

C. S. 'Todd' Andrews arrived in the Rath Camp in May 1921 as prisoner number 1569. He found that:

> Life in the camp was, in a physical sense, far from unpleasant. Indeed for the first few weeks I found it agreeably exciting meeting new people including some national personalities, exploring the library which was surprisingly good, playing football, learning the procedure for receipt of letters and parcels and examining the canteen. I had during these first few weeks the additional pleasure of receiving my internment order. The internment order was a fairly certain guarantee that the British had nothing against you for which you could be tried by court martial.[16]

For some, writing poetry helped pass the long days and nights.

Tom Behan (Rathangan), intelligence officer for Kildare, wrote a book of poems, published in 1923 after his death on the republican side in the Civil War. One, called 'My Calico Shack in Kildare', captures the atmosphere of his arrival at the Rath Camp.

In the year 'twenty-one my troubles began,
As nature from sleep was awaking;
I woke by a noise of some Houlihan boys,
Thought all demons from hell were escaping;
I listened to see what the devil it might be,
When a crowd rushed the sides and the rear
Shouting General Skinner invites you to dinner
To a calico shack in Kildare.

The leader politely told me to dress quietly,
To pack up my kit and make haste;
And lest I might bring any brandy or gin,
He searched from my boots to my waist.
Then off in a hurry, with an escort of lorry,
And armoury to bring up the rear;
Through the grand morning dew, o'er the hillside we flew
To a calico shack in Kildare.

On arrival, I found my new home was all bound
With decorations so varied and strong;
Electric lamps and barbed wire in hedgerows like briar,
A sentry en route all day long.
The guests all assembled, amongst them was [sic] mingled
The heroes of Kerry and Clare,

> From Mayo to Navan, from Longford and Cavan,
> All to dine on the plains of Kildare.
>
> The dinner once over, I was told by a soldier
> That I should be chancy and stay,
> As here every boy did fully enjoy
> The wonderful pastimes and play.
> At once I consented that I'd be contented
> To stay where this scenery fair,
> Combined with protection, disloyal correction,
> In a calico shack in Kildare.[17]

The atmosphere in the camps was not good, with frequent accusations by the prisoners of brutality. The army claimed that the internees engaged in obstruction, which took the form of refusing to answer roll call, refusing to obey orders given by British officers, 'destruction of government property and incessant clamour and complaint. The obvious and only remedy for such a course of action was to enforce obedience and good behaviour by physical violence, but such a course was not permitted by the regulations governing the treatment of internees.'[18] In an attempt to cut down on the many escape attempts by tunnelling from the Curragh, a ditch was constructed all around the camp. This ditch was filled with stagnant water, a development which 'produced vehement protest from medical authorities and much activity on the part of the local fire engine'.[19]

Todd Andrews spent nearly five months in the Rath Camp before he escaped in September 1921. He wrote of the animosity of the guards:

We had very little contact with our guards. Periodically they would patrol the camp at night. Sometimes, if they read of some successful attack by the I.R.A., they would bang on our huts with their rifle butts, wakening us and swearing at us. Sometimes they would conduct exhaustive searches of the huts during the day. They belonged to a Scottish regiment – I am not sure if it was the King's Own Scottish Borderers or the King's Own Scottish Light Infantry – but their attitude to us was very hostile. In the course of the searches they never passed without calling you a bastard or threatening you with their bayonets. They were all young conscripts who seemed to loathe us and they treated us very differently from the Lancashire Fusiliers whom I had encountered in Dublin. They were particularly offensive when they succeeded in finding an escape tunnel of which there was always at least one being dug by one or other of the companies in which the internees were organized. When a tunnel was found the whole camp was punished by the stoppage of parcels and the closure of the canteen. Once we had a fine of five shillings per man imposed because bed boards were missing; they had been used either for fuel in the stove with which each hut was furnished or as pit props for the tunnels. As not everyone got money from home, those who did refused to accept any [money] in protest. The British replied by closing the canteen and stopping the newspapers.[20]

Brigadier F. H. Vinden, a veteran of the Great War, served with the 2nd Battalion Suffolk Regiment in Ireland from 1920–22, mainly at the Curragh Camp. In extracts from his memoirs, held in the Imperial War Museum, Brigadier Vinden described the camp on his arrival and the shortcomings of guard duty for regular soldiers:

On arrival, we found an extensive hutted camp established during the war and round it we had, with the help of the Royal Engineers, to surround the camp with two ten-feet wire fences with watch towers at each corner. Aid to the civil power is one of the most unpleasant tasks which can fall to soldiers, and our colonel, Arthur Peeples, was most alert to the pitfalls for the military. If anything went wrong, it would be blamed on the soldiers and officers … Colonel Peeples wanted to avoid being in command of the regiment and at the same time be in charge of the internment camp, while the regiment only provided the guards required for it. … Colonel Peeples was correct in his forecast of troubles. The internees raised all sorts of trivial grievances and one subject which I recollect was a complaint about their parcels being opened and cakes cut. The reason was that the camp staff had found knives, files, letters and money in them.

Thinking over our time on the Curragh, I have realized how frightfully 'green' we were. We never even thought of putting agents in the cage through whom we could have hoped to get some information.[21]

The constant reports from the camp of ill-treatment, published in the Irish media, helped to sap the morale of the British military. In an effort to counter the bad press, reporters were allowed access to the camp. A *Leinster Leader* reporter was apparently given full access to the internment camp from where he made two uncensored reports on activities within the camp, which were published in the *Leader* on 21 May ('How internees spend a wet day') and 28 May 1921 ('Sport in the internment camp'). The reporter also described the internees as being in great spirits.[22]

The 'troubles' Brigadier Vinden spoke of were far less disruptive than those in the rest of the county and he found time to spend 'many an hour in evenings walking round the cage' with IRA Volunteers Desmond Fitzgerald (later a government minister) and Seán Lemass (later Taoiseach).[23]

Escapes and escape attempts led to much of the tension within the camp. An attempted tunnel escape in mid-June 1921 was foiled when a 'spy' in camp informed the military. The tunnel was all but finished when dozens of guards were brought in with a great number of trench diggers. One line of huts was isolated. It took several days before the British found the tunnel. The frustration of this discovery caused the prisoners to redouble their efforts and by the end of June there were no less than four tunnels in progress by various groups.[24] In an effort to dissuade escape attempts a warning notice was issued to the prisoners in the camp on 5 July 1921, and signed by Lieutenant and Adjutant H. F. Vinden:

Warning
The Commandant will not be responsible for the lives of any Internees seen outside their Huts or Tents between Evening Roll Call at 9 p.m. and Morning Roll Call at 7.15 a.m.[25]

This failed to have the desired effect and in a further effort to deter the prisoners, a mock shooting was enacted by the British guards of a man dressed as an internee. This seems to have had little or no effect on the internees.[26]

On 11 July a truce came into effect between the IRA and the crown forces. Despite the signing of the Truce, construction and extension works continued unabated in the Rath Camp, which included a new style of hut able to accommodate thirty men and completely surrounded by barbed wire. The Royal Engineers continued to hire more men to supplement this work at £3 1s 8d a week, substantial pay at that time.[27] Escapes by prisoners continued.

The general officer commanding the British forces in Ireland issued an order cancelling all leave on parole after an internee, James Staines, escaped from Hare Park, where he had been since March 1921. On 21 August Staines escaped by hiding in a lorry which had driven into the camp with a load of timber. Two lorries had driven into Hare Park by mistake, their proper destination being Rath Camp. Staines and a companion, seeing their opportunity, hopped into the lorries without being observed. On their way out the two lorries were examined by the guards and one of the escapees detected. Staines, however, was not noticed and jumped out of the lorry as it drove to the Rath Camp.[28]

On 9 September 1921 over sixty internees escaped from the Rath Camp on the Curragh in one of the great escapes which has entered republican folklore. When the tunnel had been discovered in mid-June, as a deterrent to further tunnelling the British had dug a trench four feet deep and four feet wide on three sides of the camp, up to three feet away from the huts. However, they did not think it necessary to make a trench on the side of the camp which held the British officers' quarters, which gave the disappointed escapees a glimmer of hope. Because of the failure of the first attempt, the second plan was a tightly held secret among the conspirators. Only six men knew of it, among them Captain Thomas Byrne and the prisoners' quartermaster, J. J. Martin. It was decided that Martin should apply for a marquee to enable him to discharge his duties. The marquee was duly delivered and made the headquarters of the escape committee. It was set up beside a hut and the new tunnel started under it. The hut was erected on concrete blocks at each end and its floor was three feet above ground. The hut's occupants did not even know that a tunnel was being constructed right under their feet.

An experienced miner, Jim Brady from Cavan, who had worked in the mines of Arigna and Pennsylvania, led the tunnel gang. His knowledge was vital. Assisted by another internee, Scottie Regan, he dug through the sandy soil using a large screwdriver and a crowbar. The soil was reasonably soft and yielded easily. The clay was pulled up in pillow covers, drawn out of the tunnel on ropes, and scattered around and closely packed under the hut. Brady dug underground for about seventy-five feet and then gradually began to work upwards. The tunnel was quite narrow, unlike the usual tunnels which required props made from bed planks. By the time it was completed, dozens knew of its existence, but not its location. It led out into No. 2 Internment Camp, a new camp, which was completed but not yet occupied. A thick barbed wire entanglement ran through the centre of this camp and had to be cut away before the men could get out through the gate, which was also heavily wired.

Thomas Byrne takes up the narrative:

I was told to go through with Joe Vize at about 12.30 a.m. [Joe Vize, had been a member of the Squad and was director of purchases, in other words head of arms smuggling. He had been arrested in Dublin in October 1920.] When our time came we made our way from the other end of the camp sticking close to the shadows of the buildings on our way. It was a foggy night and we were hoping and praying for luck. When we got to the tent we were told to wait in an adjoining hut until our turn came, as the tent could hold only a few men.

At last we got the signal and we went into the tent, lifted the flap, crawled under the hut and down we went into the tunnel. Brady's tunnel was indeed a narrow one, each man had to fight his way through, panting and wrestling with the walls. The hole was round and Vize and I, being big men, had to lever ourselves along on our elbows. The whole length of the tunnel was full of men, all screwing themselves onward in the darkness. Sometimes all movement would stop like a traffic block and we'd lie there wondering what was happening at the front. We couldn't go forward and we couldn't go back.

Just when we'd begun to think we were stuck there forever – or until we were caught and hauled out ignominiously – the movement would start again and we'd all wriggle forward another few yards. It was only later I learned the reason for the numerous halts. The lads at the exit couldn't go out until the sentry had passed on in the other direction in No Man's Land. Every time the sentry would turn his back a fresh batch would dodge out and away.

Joe Vize and I had already worked out where the wires were to be cut in the adjoining camp. We had no trouble about that and soon the way was clear. We made our way to the camp gate where another man had waited for us and the three of us walked out to the freedom of the rolling Curragh plain. We headed for the grandstand of the racecourse, which would give us our bearings. The fog held and as we melted into it we laughed as we heard behind us the sentries from the blockhouse chanting 'All's well.' All was well for us – so far.

But the fog which helped us at the start was nearly our undoing at the end, for we managed to get lost in it. And instead of making the grandstand we stumbled around the Curragh falling over whin bushes, utterly lost. After a good half-hour of this we got the fright of our lives when we discovered that our wanderings had brought us up beside the Camp and almost within the glow of the lights. Off we set again in a greater hurry than ever before and this time we found a road, which took us into Newbridge. We took the road along the Liffey and by next morning were safe in Dublin. Fifty men in all had got out that night and it took them four or five hours to get through.[29]

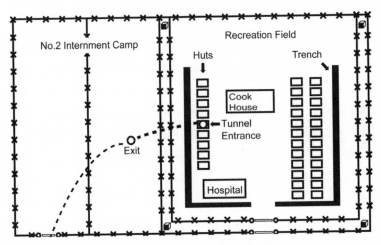

Map of Rath Camp and escape tunnel, September 1921.
(Courtesy of Brian Durney)

Seventy men were expected to escape, but the tunnel was blocked when an escapee tried to bring a suitcase on his back, causing the tunnel to partially collapse.

The fog also hindered a group of Roscommon prisoners. They ended up walking around the Curragh in circles until in

desperation they knelt down and recited the Rosary. As they finished praying they heard rooks cawing in trees nearby. Knowing
that the only trees near the camp were at the back of the racecourse grandstand, they used the cawing to guide them. Some of
them found shelter in the house of Rev. Fr Smith in Rathangan.
Local Volunteers then took them by horse and traps that evening
to Carbury, where they were treated to excellent hospitality by
the proprietor of Weyme's Hotel. From there the Roscommon
men were driven to a rendezvous near Athlone in a Leyland car
arranged by the hotel owner.[30]

The tunneller, Jim Brady, made it to Newbridge and from
there to Dublin. Another group made it to Sallins railway station
where an attendant gave them shelter until a train came along. He
flagged down the train and handed the escapees over to a guard,
who set them down safely in Dublin. Peadar Bracken, Tullamore,
and former organiser for Kildare, was found asleep in a potato
drill, near Carbury, suffering from exhaustion and frostbite.[31]

It was only at roll call the next morning that the men were
missed. The majority who escaped were from Dublin, Tullamore,
Mayo and Galway, and it was said that only one Kildare man
was included. Black and Tans, Auxiliaries and military mounted
a large-scale search throughout Kildare and the neighbouring
counties, but not one escapee was recaptured. In the camp the
internees had their privileges withdrawn for some time, but they
did not mind after the success of the escape.[32]

A further eighteen men had escaped by the end of the
following month.[33] These escapes heightened tensions and on the
night of 24 October, two of three men attempting to escape were
seriously injured by the guards, who opened fire on them.[34] In

October 1921 500 additional troops were brought into the Rath Camp in order to coerce the prisoners to give their names, etc., but there was a decisive refusal by the internees to co-operate, leading to further tension in the camp.[35]

As winter approached conditions in the camp deteriorated, with a report in the *Leinster Leader* stating that the huts in Hare Park had not been repaired since they were built in 1915, while those in the Rath Camp were of the 'felt hut class' and that 'the necessary patent tarring has not been used as far as the huts are concerned for some years, with the result that they are all in a very bad condi-tion'. By October the ground in the camp had turned into mud, often knee-deep, and there were complaints of the prisoners going hungry as food parcels were not being distributed due to the many escape attempts. However, it was reported that the men's spirit 'is as usual'.[36] These complaints led to the announcement that a 'joint investigation committee representing the republican party and the crown government' had been set up and as a result of their 'visits to the camps drastic changes were to be made in the conditions and general treatment of the interned men.'[37]

The Rath Camp and Hare Park Camp continued to function until the signing of the Anglo-Irish Treaty on 6 December 1921. Three days later the release of interned republicans began. Upwards of 450 prisoners were released from the Rath Camp on 9 December and another 700 the following day. According to the *Leinster Leader*, 'The internees looked in very good health despite their long rigorous incarceration, and were in the highest spirits.'[38] With the signing of the Treaty and the release of the internees, extension work ceased and the huts in the Rath Camp were taken down and sold off.[39]

10

WAR AND PEACE

At the beginning of 1921 there were over 50,000 troops and police in Ireland: 37,000 British troops; 13,213 RIC, including Black and Tans; 1,326 Auxiliaries and 1,134 DMP. Fifth Division of the British Army, with headquarters at the Curragh, had four brigades: the 14th Brigade (three battalions) covered Counties Carlow, Kildare, King's, Queen's and part of Wicklow. Due to commitments throughout the Empire, the British Army was seriously understrength and generally in a poor state of training. It contained a high proportion of raw recruits, who found duty in Ireland both physically and psychologically arduous.[1] On the other side, the IRA numbered around 10,000, with only 5,000 on active service at any one time. Well over 100,000 men were Volunteers at some point during 1913–21, but many were involved for only a few months and only a small fraction remained from the beginning of this period to the end.[2]

January 1921 saw the beginning of government-authorised reprisals for IRA attacks, with the destruction of seven houses at Midleton, County Cork, by order of the military governor.

Martial law, imposed in December 1920 on Cork, Kerry, Limerick and Tipperary, was extended to Clare, Wexford, Waterford and Kilkenny. The government also suspended all coroners' courts because of the large number of warrants served on members of the British forces, and replaced them with military courts of enquiry.[3]

The laying of ambushes was no longer the comparatively safe operation that it had been in the summer and autumn of 1920. A training school for guerrilla tactics had been established at the Curragh for British officers and NCOs, and both the police and troops began to move out into the country after the IRA's flying columns, who were the main perpetrators of such attacks. Reconnaissance aircraft from Baldonnel aerodrome flew over Kildare from time to time to look for ambushes or road blockings. Aircraft were also used to escort convoys of prisoners being moved to Dublin, or to cover troop or munitions trains on the lines between Kildare and the capital.[4]

Martial law, reprisals and the death penalty strengthened the resolve of the IRA. Raids, arrests, trials, curfews, harassment and attacks on crown forces increased and had become every-day happenings. In January 1921 Frank and John Corrigan from Blackrath, Curragh, were court-martialled in the Curragh Camp on a charge of having seditious literature and possessing a miniature rifle and ammunition. John Babtiste 'Babty' Maher from Athy was also held on an arms charge. Babty Maher had been a close friend of Kevin Barry and later married Barry's sister Shel.[5] Paddy Domican and Seán O'Sullivan, on the run since the August attack at Greenhills on the RIC, were arrested in Kill on 2 January 1921, when they visited the Domican home for Christmas. They were taken to Newbridge and then on to the Curragh under armed escort. With Hare Park Camp filled to capacity, most of the prisoners in the Curragh were moved to Ballykinlar Internment Camp in County Down in early January 1921. Among the twenty-five transferred from County Kildare were Seán O'Sullivan, Sallins; Jack Fitzgerald, Newbridge; Babty Maher, Athy; and Tom Harris, Prosperous. Frank Driver, Ballymore-Eustace, and Jim Smyth, Grangebeag, Dunlavin, had the honour of being the two youngest internees to remain in Hare Park in 1921. Both were in their mid-teens.[6]

In 1921 the IRA in County Kildare was engaged in many small operations that contributed to the overall struggle. There were other ways to run a 'war' than by orchestrating military attacks. If Lloyd George's aim was to make Ireland 'a hell for rebels to live in', the republican movement's aim was to make Ireland a hell for Britain to govern. The IRA's tactics and emphasis changed according to circumstances – the flying columns grew out of the need for wanted men to go on the run. At the beginning of 1921 the IRA largely moved from attacks on police barracks and ambushes to the destruction of roads, bridges and communications. The campaign to disrupt communications provided targets that were undefended and plentiful, and this shift to 'small jobs' showed a marked increase in total IRA activity, which grew month by month. In Kildare, the IRA at first performed unsatisfactorily, but soon were to receive a commendation from Chief of Staff Richard Mulcahy, in the spring of 1921.[7]

The means the Volunteers used to block the roads depended on location and circumstance; some methods were more permanent than others, such as destroying a bridge as opposed to trenching a road or felling a tree. Shallow trenches were dug across the main routes with the object of damaging British motor vehicles, which usually drove at high speed: they were remarkably effective. Tree felling also caused much delay to civilian traffic as well. Patrick O'Keefe, Kilcock, explained how painstaking these operations could be:

> I was with the Kilcock company at … the demolishing of all the bridges and culverts in and around Kilcock (we had no way of blowing up anything at that time, just pick and shovel). During those operations I was always given a gun to watch and guard from a vantage point.[8]

On the night of 2 January 1921 six masked men entered a house in Maynooth, situated between the destroyed police barracks and the college gate. The men informed the occupants that it would be burned because the military were about to take it over as a barracks. All the furniture was moved outside and the house was then set ablaze. Neighbours took in the occupants and helped store their furniture.[9]

In early January 1921 the *Leinster Leader* reported on increasing IRA activity in the county:

> … the bridges over the Liffey at Celbridge and Straffan were damaged … At Maynooth the railway bridge and canal bridges were destroyed … The bridge between Allenwood and Carbury has been destroyed, while along the big stretch of bog between Rathangan (Co. Kildare) and Edenderry (King's County) a large number of trenches were dug. In some districts in North Kildare

trees were found lying across the road. On Tuesday night last two more bridges were damaged at Kilcock and the roads blocked with trees.[10]

Seven bridges in total were damaged and Kildare County Council met to discuss the placement of night-watchmen and lights on the damaged bridges, in order to ensure the safety of the travelling public.[11] Several nights later, Cope Bridge in Leixlip, Allen Bridge and Bond Bridge near Allenwood, and Shaw's Bridge in Kilcock, were damaged by the IRA.[12]

These IRA activities resulted in reprisals by the Black and Tans. A minority of the Black and Tans were regarded as decent fellows and these were probably among the ones Ellen Gaul recalled meeting at a dance in the Town Hall in Naas and described as 'gentlemen'.[13] However, the majority were fond of a drink and this was part of their notoriety. They fought amongst themselves and with civilians in pubs, where they often refused to pay for their drink. They posed a big problem for serving RIC men, who looked on them with disdain.

Patrick Lee, owner of a grocery, hardware, drapery and public house in Calverstown, was away on business when the building housing his premises was surrounded by Black and Tans in January 1921. The occupants, Anastasia Lee, wife of Patrick, and their daughter, Elsie (9), were ordered to leave. The Black and Tans said they were going to burn the building down, as they believed the public house was being used as a meeting place for republicans. Anastasia Lee was a strong woman and vowed not to vacate the property. A local clergyman arrived on the scene, but she would not back down. The siege lasted an hour until the

Tans finally withdrew. It was believed that the premises was not torched because the shop contents, which the Tans wished to loot, would have been destroyed. The age of Elsie Lee and the intervention of the priest also helped prevent the burning.[14]

The Black and Tans were not the only ones to cause trouble, although most of the military units acquitted themselves well. Ill-disciplined actions by the military were rare in County Kildare, but on the night of 13 January 1921 two drunken soldiers from the Royal Dublin Fusiliers visited several pubs in the town of Naas, brandishing revolvers and threatening to shoot. When they discharged their revolvers in the Main Street regular RIC men arrived and arrested them. One was a Scot and the other turned out to be a Mexican![15]

On the night of 4 February the military and police raided a ball in Naas Town Hall organised by the County Kildare Farmers' Union. The sudden appearance of crown forces 'in the midst of the thronged ballroom, carrying revolvers and rifles with fixed bayonets' caused quite a stir, intimidation and 'much alarm was created amongst some of the ladies'. The military were said to be looking for a wanted man, but no search was carried out, and after a cursory look around, they left.[16]

The practice of using republicans as hostages to deter attacks on their vehicles was used by the military in the south of the county when Thomas O'Rourke and John Hayden were arrested in Athy, in the second week of February. They were placed in the vehicles for all to see and used to ensure the military's safety as they passed through Athy on their way to the Curragh Camp.[17]

On 21 February, at 10.15 p.m., a patrol consisting of one sergeant and five constables was attacked in Maynooth as it approached the local church at the junction of Kilcock and Moyglare roads. The patrol was approaching the Roman Catholic church in single file when fire was opened from the direction of a low wall. Sergeant Joseph Hughes, who was leading the group, fell, shot through the head. Four of the constables had narrow escapes. In two instances bullets passed through their overcoats and another bullet glanced off Constable Crean's ammunition pouch. The RIC returned fire and withdrew to cover. The fighting continued for over twenty minutes, when the attackers, coming under increasing pressure, escaped using the protection of the wall. The IRA group, consisting of men from North Kildare and Meath, used shotguns, rifles and revolvers in the attack. The RIC party did not pursue them. They later picked up Sergeant Hughes, who was unconscious. Police and military arrived for the follow-up search and many locals fled their homes in terror. Sergeant Hughes was brought to Dr Steeven's Hospital, Dublin, where he died the following day.

The night after the ambush a notice was posted in the town imposing a curfew between 9 p.m. and 5 a.m., by order of Colonel P. C. B. Skinner. That night, according to *The Kildare Observer*, there was 'an almost complete evacuation of Maynooth by the civilian population … who sought refuge elsewhere through fear of reprisals'. Sergeant Hughes was thirty-four and a native of Wolfhill, near Ballylinan, County Laois. He had twelve years' service in the RIC and had previously been a postman. He was described as a 'very popular man' and had spent most of his service in County Kildare, only recently arriving in Maynooth from Naas Barracks after his promotion to sergeant. A guard of honour from Naas, with Inspector Supple and DI Fallon in charge, met the funeral cortège at Sallins railway station as the coffin was conveyed by train to Athy station. In Naas, the windows in businesses were shuttered or had their blinds drawn, as requested by the local RIC. All business premises in Athy were closed between 10 a.m. and noon by direction of the police. A large crowd assembled for Sergeant Hughes' funeral to Ballylinan. A guard of honour of about twenty police marched with arms reversed to Ballylinan and from there to the graveyard.[18]

The areas around the County Kildare garrison towns were particularly difficult for the IRA to operate in, and there were other factors to consider. Most operations had to be sanctioned from GHQ in Dublin, who ordered when and where lines of communications were to be cut. GHQ wanted the main roads to remain open for the sending and receiving of orders, except when they were planning some big operation. If there was increased activity along these roads it would mean constant checkpoints and the risk of IRA orders being intercepted.

Smaller roads could still be targeted. Athgarvan Company, from their base on the edge of the Curragh, by order of GHQ, carried out a small campaign of subversion and harassment against the crown forces by trenching roads and cutting telephone lines. Soldiers and civilians from the camp and Newbridge Barracks were enticed to procure weapons, explosives and ammunition for the IRA, in addition to supplying intelligence reports on troop strengths and movements.[19]

Lack of training and equipment was a constant handicap. An attempt in early 1921 to blow up the Limerick Road Bridge outside Naas failed due to inexperience. Mick Sheehan (Newbridge) and Bill Jones (Athgarvan) met several Volunteers from Naas for the operation. It was assumed that as Jones was a war veteran he would know what to do, but his experience with the Connaught Rangers during the Great War was in trench warfare and he knew nothing about blowing up bridges, which was usually the work of engineers. Sheehan wrapped sticks of dynamite in newspaper and stuck fuses in them to set the explosive alight, but without detonators it was useless. Later, when Mick Sheehan grew more experienced in the use of explosives, he learned how to blow up a bridge properly.[20]

Athy produced huge numbers of recruits for the British Army during the Great War so it is perhaps surprising that it was a particularly active area during the War of Independence. Roads were regularly trenched or blocked with trees and bridges damaged by the local IRA. On 16 March the local police posted regulations ordering a curfew from 9 p.m. to 5 a.m. in the districts of Tullamore, Mountmellick, Cloneygown and Athy No. 1 District, and prohibited the Tuesday market in Athy. A notice from 'The competent military authorities' was posted in the town warning that in any area in which damage was caused to the local infrastructure the holding of fairs and markets would be stopped. The market of the following Tuesday took place, although the curfew started at the earlier time of 8 p.m. Due to continued republican activity, the Athy fair was prohibited on numerous occasions.[21]

The Auxiliaries passed through Naas on two occasions in March en route from the south and halted in the town. On the first occasion, 3 March, they pulled up their vehicle in Poplar Square and searched several people, including some ex-servicemen. They also raided businesses in Newbridge the same week and lined up people on the street to be searched. On the morning of 18 March the Auxiliaries halted their half-a-dozen lorries in the town centre, where they caught sight of an inscription in Irish on the door of the room of the Town Hall that was formerly used as a Sinn Féin club. They entered the building by a back window and searched some of the rooms, removing a number of Volunteer caps, some armbands with the inscription IV and a large republican flag. The cadets put the caps on and the flag was tied high up on the protective cage of one of the lorries. The Irish inscription above the door was painted over with red paint and 'God save the King' and 'Up the RIC' were painted on the front of the Town Hall close to the club room. After spending a couple of hours in the town the party climbed back into their lorries and drove off towards Dublin. The paint on the inscription was removed a few minutes after their departure while it was still wet.[22]

One particular ambush planned by the IRA in Kildare was a complete failure. On 20 March fifty-five men, armed with seven rifles and thirty shotguns, gathered to ambush a police patrol near the Hill of Allen. An RIC tender, containing a reported twelve policemen, was expected to pass from Kildare that evening. All the available members from the Prosperous, Allen, Robertstown and Allen Companies were mobilised to ambush the lorry. The RIC tender did not arrive until late in the evening and a number of the men had been demobilised. Those remaining opened fire but, while fire was returned, the vehicle did not stop and there were no injuries on either side. The military and police were very active in the area after this episode and a number of men were arrested, including Commandant Michael Fitzgerald, Allen Cross,

Kilmeague, OC Allen Company, who was interned at the Rath Camp, where he remained until after the Treaty was signed.[23]

The inexperience of the Kildare men involved in the Hill of Allen ambush was clear. By the beginning of 1921 the RIC knew that the IRA was capable of conducting fairly sophisticated ambushes and their intelligence network was competent enough to avoid such a simple error as using the same route on a return journey. One of the countermeasures employed by crown forces was higher driving speeds and a reluctance to stop. Yet the Kildare men had not, for example, made a serious attempt to halt the vehicle by blocking or trenching the road. Chief of Staff Richard Mulcahy was not happy with the outcome and did not want to see large groups of men, like those at Allen, becoming involved in confrontations with the enemy before the necessary training had been undertaken. He wrote to Commandant Michael Smyth, OC 2nd Kildare Battalion:

> I am glad to see that you are developing officers who are not afraid to handle such a large body of men as 55, but the idea of this sudden development makes me rather nervous. I would prefer to see your men trained on jobs that would require not more than half the number ... It would be very bad if such a force got themselves, through want of training or want of [?] into a position in which they got a big defeat.[24]

GHQ was scathing of the role played by many of the IRA units outside Dublin and the south. A letter from Mulcahy to the OC 7th Brigade emphasised the importance of his region in suppressing the British forces. Mulcahy understood that the focus of Kildare's activity should be less on military confrontation than on containing the enemy by the destruction of communications:

> ... in Dublin-Curragh region [the] English have permanently quartered between ⅓ and ½ of their total armed strength in Ireland, and all their vital lines have to pass through the narrow bottle-neck between Celbridge and Brittas (Co. Wicklow). This is a sufficient reason to bring all possible pressure to bear on them in the area – despite poor quality of units immediately available there.[25]

As result of this and several earlier communiqués, activity was stepped up in Kildare. On the night of 23 March, six out of the nine companies in the 1st Battalion were particularly busy: A Company felled two large trees on the road to the Curragh Camp; D Company trenched the main Dublin to Naas road at Johnstown; F Company damaged the canal bridge at Naas; G Company damaged the canal bridge at Blackwood and trenched three roads; and I Company trenched the main road from Naas to Kilcullen.[26]

The successful operations were not without their consequences, however. Six of the fourteen or so members of I Company (Two-Mile-House) were picked up within a week. Tom Fitzharris, Mullacash, recalled:

> The speed with which the lads dug trenches and felled trees greatly impressed us all. I remember seeing the trench they made on the Oldtown road ... It was quite deep and poplar trees were positioned on either side of it. Further down the Kilcullen road at Berney's, nine beech trees were used to block the road.

The day all the boys were caught will always remain in my memory. My brother, Dan, and I were bringing the ponies for watering down to the stream … on the Oldtown side of Mullacash Crossroads when, suddenly, the place was swarming with 'Tanners.' They stopped us and demanded to know where we were going. When we told them, two of the Tanners were detailed to accompany us to the stream. They marched on either side of the ponies to ensure that we didn't race off to raise the alarm. However, it was already too late for some of the boys. Tom and Mick Fitzharris, Jack Timmons and Jack Hickey had been apprehended. They were lined up against the wall in their shirt sleeves, while the rest of the soldiers started digging all around in a fruitless search for arms and ammunition.

Once the ponies had refreshed themselves, the Tans told us to clear off. Without a thought for his own safety, Dan leapt on a pony and galloped off to warn Jack Fitzharris who was doing a bit of gardening down at our place, but Jack had already left and was down in Mrs. Mooney's. Andy Byrne and the rest of the lads made a dash for Dunnstown Wood and remained there until it was safe to come out of hiding.

Unfortunately, Andy's luck was about to run out. About a week later, he was out in the garden sowing potatoes when the Tans swooped. They took him into custody, without even giving him time to get his coat. The next to be caught was Tom O'Hara. He wasn't a very active man, so when the Tans told him to start running, he was more than a little apprehensive. 'We'll count to fifty,' they said. 'Sure, if you're out of range, you'll live.' He ran![27]

The dramatic rise in small jobs was a direct result of pressure from GHQ. Their earlier tactics of not disrupting communication had changed and offensive activity was stepped up, with GHQ specifically ordering the Kildare IRA to disrupt communications by trenching more roads, destroying bridges, breaking railway lines, raiding mails and cutting telegraph lines. These activities virtually paralysed transport and communications in the county and were a great source of frustration to the military and police. Road trenching was a major success, as roads in the county became almost completely impassable. In March alone there were twenty-two occasions where roads were trenched. This activity of the Kildare IRA was crucial to the national campaign, as it prevented effective British action from the Curragh Camp and disrupted military travel to the south and west.

On 20 April Gearóid Ó Sullivan, adjutant-general of the IRA, reported his satisfaction to Richard Mulcahy that the Kildare IRA was stepping up their activities and thought it would be well to send them encouragement. On 22 April Mulcahy wrote to Michael Smyth, OC 2nd Battalion: 'I want to express my appreciation of the fact that you are getting systematically to work.' Mulcahy's note suggested the perceived importance of effective intelligence work and the destruction of the enemy's vital communications links to the IRA's overall campaign.[28]

One downed bridge or trenched road did not normally cut off communications with the surrounding countryside. It was the cumulative effect of so many such operations that made the difference. Countermobility operations took time to develop. The true effects of this essentially non-violent campaign took time to surface, but by May 1921 British military and police commanders had begun to complain about their inability to manoeuvre due to the state of the roads. By June so many roads and bridges had been blocked or destroyed that even mounted cavalry had difficulty travelling. One cavalry officer, when encountering such difficulty while riding on an offensive drive with the 10th Lancers and the 12th Hussars, asked the commander: 'If it is like this within twenty miles of the Curragh, what is it going to be like in Cork?'[29]

Many of the Kildare IRA were itching to get into action with the crown forces and resented the role they had to play with their local units. Some were active with the Dublin Brigade, others elsewhere. Pat O'Carroll (Naas), for example, was sent to the newly formed Kildare/Wicklow flying column, comprising twelve men from Kildare 2nd Battalion, which included parts of County Wicklow. The column was evenly divided between Kildare and Wicklow Volunteers and operated mostly in County Wicklow. It was under the command of ex-British soldier Martin O'Neill (Ballymore-Eustace), former OC B Company, 2nd Kildare Battalion. Pat O'Carroll had come to notice when tasked with the dismantling of the telephones at Punchestown grandstand on the eve of the annual races:

This order was duly complied with, and on the Thursday following at a Battalion Council Meeting at Two-Mile-House I was appointed to the newly-formed column. The column headquarters were located at Baltiboys, Co. Wicklow. Proceeding at once to Ballymore in company with Jack Winders we occupied an empty house with the appellation of 'Shamrock Lodge' and next day went to Blessington. Here we called on Tom Byrne who provided us with supplies of bedding and other articles. These we took with us to Baltiboys where the column was under command of Martin Neill [sic], Ballymore. A fortnight's leisurely life followed and then a raid on the mails carried by the Dublin Blessington Steam Tram took place.[30]

In early May, when the column was disbanded and Wicklow Volunteers attached themselves to the South Dublin Brigade, they demanded half the rifles and ammunition, but this was refused as the rifles were the property of the Kildare companies and were purchased from British soldiers at the Curragh Camp and Newbridge.[31]

The funeral of Seán (Jack) O'Sullivan gave local people the chance to express their support for the republican campaign. On 3 May 1921 O'Sullivan died in Ballykinlar Internment Camp from the effects of a beating he received when he was arrested. Indeed, Ballykinlar Camp was notorious for brutality: two prisoners from County Westmeath were shot dead for going too near the wire. O'Sullivan was a native of Tipperary but lived at Sherlockstown, Sallins. He was employed by Thomas Broughall of Kill in 1913 and soon after its formation joined Kill Company of the Volunteers. After the Greenhills ambush the police made particular inquiries about him. He succeeded in eluding capture until St Stephen's Day 1920, when the house of a friend he was visiting was unexpectedly surrounded and raided, and he and a comrade were captured. On the way to Naas RIC Barracks they were badly beaten and O'Sullivan received internal injuries. The injuries were aggravated by his subsequent treatment and the long journey to Ballykinlar in January 1921, on board a British battleship from Dublin. An account in the *Leinster Leader*, 2 April 1966, by a contemporary of O'Sullivan, stated:

> Life in an internment camp such as that at Ballykinlar did not tend to relieve the sufferings he endured as a consequence of the treatment to which he already had been subjected but it

was hoped by his fellow prisoners that his youth and robust construction would bring back his former health and vitality. For a time his buoyant nature and good spirits encouraged this hope, but it was at length realised that his injuries were fatal. He wasted away and lingered on in suffering until, on May 3, the end came. Dr. O'Higgins and Rev. Fr. Burbage, who were among the internees, did everything possible for the dying youth and the ministrations of the priest afforded him such consolation that his death was a happy one.

Kildare men in the camp mounted a guard over the remains, pending the arrival of men from his adopted county to convey them there. The coffin in which the body was placed was made by his fellow prisoners and bore the inscription: 'Goodbye, Jack. From your comrades, the Irish Volunteers in Ballykinlar Internment Camp, Co. Down'. It was covered with a republican flag and, when the escort from Kildare arrived, was borne to the entrance gates of the camp between double files of prisoners who lined the passage from the temporary mortuary. The pall bearers were Tom Traynor, Tom Patterson, Jimmy Whyte and Jack Fitzgerald, interned members of 2nd Kildare Battalion. As the remains were being conveyed to the entrance gates, the British military guard attempted to snatch the republican flag from the coffin, but the internees prevented them and, getting possession of the flag first, passed it rapidly down the long ranks of prisoners to safety.

The coffin was handed over to the escort from Kildare, placed in a motor hearse and brought back to Kill, where it was carried into the parish church to remain overnight. On 6 May the funeral took place to St Corban's Cemetery, Naas, where the local UDC had donated a plot of ground for the interment of O'Sullivan's remains. Thirty-six men of Kill Company, IRA, turned out to give O'Sullivan a military funeral. They marched behind the hearse, which had a guard of honour of six men on either side, followed by a contingent of Fianna Éireann and Sinn Féin, and a large attendance of the general public. Despite the presence of 200 military, police and Black and Tans, 2,000 mourners walked with the funeral party the four miles from Kill to St Corban's Cemetery. Seven Volunteers from Kill who attended O'Sullivan's funeral were picked up shortly after.[32]

Early on the afternoon of 16 May, eight young IRA men living in the Barrowhouse area of Athy left their homes and walked to a prearranged meeting place in the graveyard adjoining Barrowhouse church. They were Joe Maher, Cullinagh; Joe Ryan, Kilmoroney; Paddy Dooley, Killabbin, Maganey; Jim Lacey, Augharea; and James O'Connor, Mick Maher, Jack O'Brien and Joe Lacey, Barrowhouse. They were all members of B Company, 5th Carlow Battalion, based in the Barrowhouse area. Many Kildare units in the south of the county were attached to Carlow Brigade, which took in some areas of South Kildare and Wicklow. A Company, Athy, B Company, Barrowhouse, and C Company, Castledermot, were attached to Carlow 5th Battalion. These IRA men intended to ambush RIC men stationed in Ballylinan, who regularly travelled on the road between Maganey and Ballylinan. A spy in the local police barracks had revealed that a police patrol was expected to pass through Barrowhouse that afternoon on its way from the Ballylinan RIC Barracks to Maganey. On the previous night arms and ammunition had been brought from Castledermot and delivered to Joe Maher, who was the leader of the Barrowhouse men.

Seven of the men, armed mostly with shotguns, lay in wait, while one acted as a lookout. The police were late, however, and as the five-man patrol approached on bicycles the doors of the nearby school opened and dozens of children rushed out. The policemen dismounted and walked past the waiting IRA men, surrounded on both sides by boys and girls on their way home. There was now no possibility of carrying out the ambush, so the IRA men moved across the fields to cut off the patrol further up the road.

At the side of the roadway at Mountbrook the IRA launched their attack, but it was a disaster. The shotguns were inaccurate and it was thought that the ammunition was damp and therefore ineffective. One policeman was hit by pellets in the face and head. The RIC reacted quickly, jumping off their bicycles into ditches and replying with deadly and accurate fire from their Lee-Enfield rifles. Volunteers James O'Connor and Jim Lacey were instantly shot dead. O'Connor was hit in the neck and Lacey in the side. When his body was recovered, his shotgun was still in his hands. The remaining IRA men, helpless in the face of superior RIC firepower, withdrew.

The bodies of O'Connor and Lacey were taken to the RIC barracks in Ballylinan and not released until the following Tuesday. The night of the attack and the following morning arrests were made in the area. About 1 a.m. a party of ten partly disguised policemen arrived in Barrowhouse. Shots were fired throughout the district and the inhabitants terrorised until daylight. Black and Tans went to the home of John Lynch, Barrowhouse, captain of the local IRA Company, demanding the whereabouts of rifles used in the day's attack. The Tans gave the occupants ten minutes to clear out and take whatever furniture and valuables they could carry. They then sprinkled petrol throughout the house and set it ablaze. Another house, used as a Sinn Féin office, was demolished. On their departure from the area, the policemen burned a quantity of hay and straw belonging to Mr Lyons.

Crown forces, including police, arrived the next day and asked who the raiders were. The police denied all knowledge of the previous night's raiders, even though the men had spoken with English accents. On Thursday morning, after 11 o'clock Mass, O'Connor and Lacey were buried at Barrowhouse. Both men were twenty-one and had been born, christened and killed on the same date, and buried in the same grave. Their coffins were carried from the church on the shoulders of local men to the nearby graveyard. As the coffins were lowered into the grave, a lone trumpeter sounded the 'Last Post'. Several weeks later, armed and masked men burned the residence of a policeman in Ballylinan in retaliation for the burnings in Barrowhouse. The constable was, luckily for him, in the barracks at the time.[33]

In late April and early May the IRA reorganised along the lines of a regular army. Sixteen divisions were formed based on region. Nine brigades, which covered Counties Meath, Kildare, north Offaly, south Louth, east Cavan and part of Westmeath, formed the First Eastern Division, with the 7th Brigade – headquartered in Naas – being responsible for most of County Kildare.[34] Because of the fortification of RIC barracks, the IRA had switched its main focus of attack to ambushing police patrols. As at Barrowhouse, the IRA waited at suitable ambush sites for small parties of RIC, who were on foot or on bicycles. On 17 May an RIC patrol travelled between Lanesborough and

Ballymahon from Longford town through a wild and lonely part of the county. They had to negotiate trenched and barricaded roads and were ambushed near Rathcline. They took shelter in a nearby cottage and held off the attackers. However, three constables were wounded and one, Edmund Kenyon (22) from Kilcock, County Kildare, was killed. Kenyon was an ex-soldier who had joined the RIC just seven months earlier and had only recently returned to duty after his marriage. His body was later taken to Dublin by train.

The following day a police patrol was ambushed in the town of Letterkenny, County Donegal. This resulted in the wounding of a sergeant and the death of a constable, Albert Carter (21), a single man from Carbury, County Kildare. He had only four months' police service, having been a farmer before joining the RIC. After a service in the Protestant church in Letterkenny, Carter's remains were carried by his former comrades through the town, flanked by other policemen. The coffin was then placed into a motor hearse and taken home. His brother travelled along with it. Albert Carter's remains were buried in Kilmeague.[35]

On 3 May 1921 the Better Government of Ireland Act had nominally come into force, effectively partitioning the country with two parliaments. Elections of members to sit in these parliaments took place in the southern twenty-six counties on 19 May and in the northern six counties on 24 May. The twenty-six counties were entitled to send thirty-three representatives to Westminster, while the six counties could send thirteen. The republican movement refused to recognise the act and decreed that, as a demonstration of the people's will, the elections were to be regarded as elections for the Second Dáil of a united country.

Refusing to recognise the Home Rule parliaments, the Dáil had decided to use the British election machinery as a cheap and convenient way of electing the Second Dáil. At the election Sinn Féin candidates (124) were returned unopposed in every southern constituency save the unionist stronghold of Trinity College, which elected four members.[36]

There was a small attendance at the formal declaration of the result of the parliamentary elections at Naas courthouse. The sub-sheriff for County Kildare, Charles Daly, declared: 'elected to serve in the Southern Parliament of Ireland' on behalf of Counties Kildare and Wicklow: Domhnall Ua Buachalla, Art O'Connor, Robert C. Barton, Erskine Childers and Christopher M. Byrne.[37]

Security operations by the military and police increased as the number of IRA operations mounted. In June the barracks in Athy was attacked and a military car hijacked and burned near Castledermot, the attackers escaping with a dispatch bag. The barracks at Kilcullen was also attacked, although there were no casualties. Courts martial were held regularly at Beresford (now Ceannt) Barracks of people found in possession of arms or seditious literature. On 5 June fifteen army lorries carrying military and police arrived at the sports field in Athy, where a sports meeting was being held in aid of the local feis. Sentries were posted and the people rounded up and questioned. The event was not allowed to proceed and three men were taken to the police barracks for further questioning. A cordon was placed around the town and remained in position for an hour.[38]

On 13 June 1921 the IRA shot dead an ex-soldier at Kilboggan House, near Nurney. Michael Power (40) had served in the British Army for over a year as a sapper, being too old for active service. Originally from Kilkenny, in the summer of 1920 he was living with his wife, Elizabeth, a local woman, and four young children at Brownstown, Curragh. While investigating cattle stealing in the Curragh area that summer, the local IRA had arrested the ex-soldier. One night fifteen men surrounded his cottage and attacked the door. Power immediately went down and opened it, and two masked men armed with revolvers entered. They asked if he was Power and then took him away, half-dressed. He returned several hours later and told his wife he had been taken before a republican court and tried for larceny. He was sentenced to leave the country for a period of twelve months on the following Monday. Power obtained married quarters in the Curragh Camp and employment with the Royal Engineers that September. When questioned by the camp authorities he allegedly named the people involved, as some of them were living locally.

The following April Elizabeth Power had visited her sister at the house of Henry Scully in Kilboggan where she was employed. Michael Power had later joined his wife and left about 7 p.m. About two hours later four men, two of them masked and armed with revolvers, arrived at the house and asked Mrs Power where her husband was. She told them he had gone home. After searching the house they left.

On 13 June Mrs Power again visited her sister at Kilboggan House accompanied by her husband. The owner of the house, Henry Scully, told Michael Power that he should not stay too long as he was in danger. Power said he was going outside to collect some eggs and would be back in a few minutes. Mrs Power was upstairs at the time, and after her husband had left she noticed three men approaching the house. When she observed the man in the centre put a white handkerchief over his face she became alarmed and hurriedly went downstairs. The IRA men approached Power as he was leaving the stable and the one with the handkerchief shot him three times at close range with a small calibre pistol. Power fell face downwards, hit in the chest, collarbone and groin. He was unconscious when his wife found him. She remained beside him until he died about thirty minutes later. He never spoke. The police, with an escort of military, arrived some hours later and took the body back to the Curragh. Mrs Power and her children emigrated to Scotland the following year.[39]

Research has shown that a large proportion of those killed by the IRA during the War of Independence as spies were arrested, tried and convicted on the flimsiest of evidence. Very few were proved to be actual 'spies'. Often there were underlying reasons for their deaths. Michael Smyth recalled:

A man, named Power of Kilboggan, Suncroft was questioned about robberies in the area, but before he could be arrested he sought refuge on Curragh Camp, where he gave information concerning the I.R.A. He was kept under the protection of the British military at Curragh Camp. When he left camp to return home on one occasion he was arrested, tried, found guilty and executed. There was considerable enemy activity around Suncroft after the execution, but no arrests were made. Some other spies, including a woman, were under observation, but they, too, took refuge in Curragh Camp.

At a meeting of the battalion council at the end of 1920 the members were perturbed at the number of arrests taking place in the battalion area – especially of battalion and company officers. It was believed that there were informers and spies in the area. Some persons were mentioned as suspects.

As a result of a visit by Volunteers to the house of a man suspected of giving information, he was fired on and mortally wounded but first attacked the party with a slane (a type of scythe) and struck one of the Volunteers on the head. A number of men were arrested in the area after this incident – but none of them were members of the I.R.A.[40]

On Derby Day, 17 June, at the Curragh the military held up cars going to the races to look for permits, while in Kildare town, after the races, armoured cars surrounded the railway station. Racing at Kilcock was also disrupted when soldiers, Auxiliaries and police rounded up some of the punters. All males were searched, though no arrests were made. The crown forces left, taking a quantity of liquor with them. The races were called off by order of the officer in command. In Robertstown, the annual sports day was cancelled by the military, causing the organising committee to complain about the waste of effort and loss of finance. In the Curragh area, following a widespread spate of road blocking, the army commandeered local young men to clear the trees. A football match between Cappagh and Kilcock had to be postponed when crown forces arrested the Cappagh captain and four players. Later, Caragh lost the county final to St Conleth's on an objection, because they excluded C. McCarthy from the referee's list as his 'personal liberty would be endangered by his appearance on the football field'.[41]

By mid-1921 the Kildare IRA was perturbed at the number of arrests taking place in the 2nd Battalion area, especially of battalion and company officers. It was believed that there were informers and spies in the area. People loyal to the government or those who did not share the views of the republican movement were a constant source of worry to republicans. Some persons, rightly or wrongly, were identified as suspects.

Several men called at the house of Philip Dunne, Grange-higgin, Allen, on the night of 14 June. Philip (30) lived with his mother and two sisters in a cottage on a small holding. He earned his living selling turf and working for local farmers. The object of the visit is unclear, but the family repulsed the men with spades and other implements. Two nights later two IRA men called at the Dunne house and during a conversation Philip Dunne attacked them with a slash-hook, striking one on the arm. A number of shots were fired and Philip was shot. Two bullets also hit Mrs Anne Dunne (70) as she stepped between her son and the raiders. The two managed to reach the house of a local priest some distance away. Philip died some hours later, while Mrs Dunne was taken to the Kildare Infirmary. She survived. The RIC arrived next day and arrested five men from the area. They were removed to Mountjoy Jail. According to Paddy Sheehan (Newbridge), the men who had shot Dunne were not local, but were from Athgarvan Company.

Philip Dunne was buried in Allen Cemetery on 19 June. The only persons present at the interment were Rev. Fr Bennett, CC; Dr Blake, the priest's servant; the deceased's brother and a cousin. According to *The Kildare Observer*, 'The shocking affair has created consternation in the locality'. However, over ninety years later the full story is still unclear. The Dunne family are adamant that Philip was not shot for spying, but that a land issue was at the root of the incident. The men who killed him had possibly been called in to arbitrate and it was Dunne's violent reaction that resulted in his fatal shooting and the wounding of his mother.[42]

The annual republican pilgrimage to Bodenstown graveyard, which takes place every third Sunday in June, was banned. The military authorities announced that it would 'give rise to grave disorder and […] cause undue demands made on the police and military'. All roads leading to the graveyard were blocked by military checkpoints manned by fully equipped troops. However, there were no attempts to reach the graveyard.[43]

While rumours of peace circulated, the struggle continued: two bridges on the main road between Monasterevin and Maryborough and on the road between Monasterevin and Portarlington were damaged, and a rural postman was held up and relieved of his letters. Belfast goods were seized in Milltown and boycotted goods burned in shops in Robertstown and Kilmeague, while three large stacks of flax belonging to a Belfast firm were destroyed by fire at Riverstown, near Monasterevin, on 26 June. Sergeant McCarthy of the RIC fired three shots at fleeing men, after a large stone was thrown through an upstairs window of his house on the Fair Green, Naas. Two nights later the windows in the homes of three republican families were broken. On the night of 31 June the post office in Newbridge and the sub-post offices at Rathangan and Athy were raided. Systematic raids on post offices at Johnstownbridge, Donadea, Clane, Enfield, Robertstown and Carbury followed.[44]

Armed men visited the residence of Mr D. More O'Farrell, DL, JP, at Kildangan Castle, near Monasterevin, and at gunpoint made him promise not to sign any more summonses. More O'Farrell was a magistrate for the Monasterevin petty sessions district. Volunteers also removed the mail bag from Monasterevin railway station and locked the postman in a hut. The letters were returned a few days later, censored and marked 'Passed by the I.R.A.'

Road trenching and tree felling had become a huge nuisance, leading *The Kildare Observer* to remark that the 'road from Kilcullen to Athy is perhaps the most uncomfortable in the county to traverse at present'. Fallen trees also blocked many byroads in the district. The village of Robertstown was completely isolated when the IRA sawed down dozens of telegraph poles.[45]

Crown forces surprised a party of IRA men on 2 July as they attempted to mine the railway bridge at Hazelhatch, near Celbridge. The men were members of the Meath/North Kildare flying column led by Paddy Mullaney, Leixlip. Among the Kildare men with the column were John Cotter, Tom Cardwell and Jack O'Connor. The column was planning to derail a British troop train coming from Dublin, when a routine patrol of the South Lancashire Regiment appeared in a military vehicle. In the ensuing firefight six of the IRA men were wounded and several from Meath were captured. Jack O'Connor was later picked up and interned in the Curragh. The military found six landmines in position on the railway line. They also captured the following material:

Guncotton and gelignite
100 yards of cable
2 electrical cells
1 box of detonators

1 electrical exploder

1 Ford car

5 bicycles

1 rifle

2 shotguns

Approx. 300 rounds of .303 ammunition

32 rounds of revolver ammunition

1 mail bag full of letters.[46]

Commandant Michael Smyth, who had been promoted to OC 7th Brigade, 1st Eastern Division, on its formation the previous month, was arrested on a charge of possessing arms on 7 July. With him was Bill Jones, lieutenant of engineering. Jones had been on the run for some time. Both men were armed, but they were surprised by a party of Black and Tans at Two-Mile-House. They were beaten by the police and brought to Newbridge Military Barracks, where they were detained until 13 July. They were then transferred to Hare Park. They were brought to Mountjoy Jail for trial in October and held there until the general amnesty of 14 January 1922. Jones underwent a hunger strike while in Mountjoy.[47]

On the night of 7 July, the worst tragedy of the War of Independence in County Kildare occurred. Armed IRA Volunteers visited the extensive premises of the Army and Navy Canteen at Ballymany, Newbridge, where they held up the caretaker, William Doran, while a quantity of goods was taken out to a waiting car. The men sprinkled the remaining goods with paraffin oil in an attempt to render them useless. Doran was then released and went upstairs to the living accommodation to his wife, Bridget (34), and three children. However, as the men left Doran came down to check the premises holding a lighted candle. It was thought he let it fall, resulting in a fireball explosion, which blew down the wall and set the house on fire. William Doran, Jnr, escaped, although his clothes were set on fire. Bridget Doran threw her ten-month-old baby from a window to her husband and went back to rescue her stepson, thirteen-year-old John, but the floor gave way. The fire brigade from the Curragh and Newbridge Barracks were quickly on the scene, but their efforts were of little avail. A number of the walls left standing were pulled down owing to their dangerous condition. The charred remains of Mrs Doran and her stepson were recovered the next day and brought to the mortuary in the military barracks.[48]

By the summer both sides were moving towards peace. The only plan to end the conflict on the British side was either maintain the status quo, which was failing, or full-scale war. However, the government could not send any more troops to Ireland to implement the latter, because the British Empire simply did not have enough men to meet its global commitments. The Irish conflict was costing Britain around £20 million annually and, more importantly, the actions of the Black and Tans and Auxiliaries had become a great embarrassment. Even King George V was known to be acutely distressed by the treatment of his 'Irish subjects' and had appealed for peace when he opened the Northern Ireland parliament in June.

The IRA, too, was in some difficulty. It was short of arms and had lost many of its most experienced members either to imprisonment or death as a result of the conflict. Both sides were anxious to end the conflict and British Prime Minister Lloyd

George invited Éamon de Valera, and any colleagues he should choose, to meet him in London. Arthur Griffith and several other prominent republicans, including Robert Barton, were released from jail, and delighted crowds cheered General Macready to his meeting with the Irish leaders at the Mansion House on 8 July. The terms of a truce were decided at General Macready's headquarters, Parkgate Street, Dublin, the following day and were to come into effect three days later.[49] The Dáil Publicity Department then issued the following statement:

On behalf of the British Army it is agreed as follows:
1. No incoming troops, RIC, and Auxiliary Police and munitions, and no movements for military purposes of troops and munitions, except maintenance drafts.
2. No provocative display of forces, armed or unarmed.
3. It is understood that all provisions of this truce apply to the martial law area equally with the rest of Ireland.
4. No pursuit of Irish officers or men or war material or military stores.
5. No secret agents, noting description or movements, and no interference with the movements of Irish persons, military or civil, and no attempts to discover the haunts or habits of Irish officers and men. Note:- This supposes the abandonment of Curfew restrictions.
6. No pursuit or observance of lines of communication or connection.

Note: – there are other details connected with courts martial, motor permits, and ROIR to be agreed later.

On behalf of the Irish Army it is agreed that:
a) Attacks on Crown Forces and civilians to cease.

b) No provocative displays of forces, armed or unarmed.

c) No interference with Government or private property.

d) To discountenance and prevent any action likely to cause disturbance of peace which might necessitate military interference.[50]

The terms came into effect at noon on Monday 11 July. Though operations by the crown forces virtually ceased from the truce conference, IRA activity continued up to the very last minute. A general order from the 1st Eastern Division to the headquarters of the 7th Brigade on 9 July said that although hostilities would cease in two days it was imperative that:

> ... a good stroke be made at the enemy before then. Such strokes will it is believed strengthen the hands of our representatives in the making of a definite peace. You will therefore hit anywhere and everywhere you can within your area before 12 noon on Monday. All spies of whom you may have already been advised of are to be executed also before said hour on Monday.[51]

Despite the orders from HQ to keep the pressure up there was little activity in County Kildare. The only reported incidents were the trenching of roads in Athy, which continued up to the morning of the Truce, and the firing of shots near the RIC barracks.

In Newbridge, Kildare, Athy and Monasterevin, there were bonfires surrounded by joyous crowds of singing people to celebrate the signing of the Truce. In Athy, people were out strolling, taking advantage of the relaxation of the curfew. That weekend the *Leinster Leader* reported:

The Armistice has been splendidly observed on all sides throughout Kildare. When in Celbridge one could see everyone on the point of extending congratulations and the same may be said all round. In Droichead Nua and in Kildare areas there was a very good feeling shown and not the slightest matter occurred to mar the peaceful air which was evident the moment the entry of the peace had been made.[52]

The War of Independence was officially over. It had caused over 1,300 deaths, the majority of which occurred after the arrival of the Black and Tans and Auxiliaries. Estimates vary, but the figure most often agreed is 405 police, 162 military, 450 civilians and around 300 republicans.

11

TRUCE AND TREATY

The Truce had elements of victory and defeat for both sides. Neither side wanted to prolong the fight further. For Irish republicans it had led to a unique level of success not managed by earlier rebellions. The British government, which had always before been able to crush armed Irish rebellion, had been forced to seek terms with the IRA. However, the British forces had not been driven out of Ireland and continued to have a presence on Irish soil for years to come. Moreover, the Truce was much more damaging to the IRA's future capabilities than it was to that of regular professional forces. Key men, such as Michael Collins, had to come out into the open. Also, with the relaxing of tension the population became less ready to resume the burdens of war, which affected the republicans' cause during the Civil War.

While recruiting for the RIC stopped on 11 July 1921, recruitment for the IRA continued throughout the Truce. Between July and December the ranks of the IRA swelled dramatically, with many expecting a return to hostilities rather than a peace settlement. Some estimates put active strength in July 1921 as low as 3–5,000 men, but this had increased to 72,000 by the signing of the Anglo-Irish Treaty in December. While there was major resentment from the rank and file towards these new recruits, who were contemptuously labelled 'Trucers' or 'Trucileers', the IRA leadership wanted to expand and were pleased at the opportunity to train and re-arm.[1]

The Kildare 7th Brigade, comprising six battalions, was formed three days before the Truce, with Thomas Lawler of Halverstown, Naas as Brigade OC. Its total strength was about 1,600 men. On 11 July 1921, the day the Truce came into effect, Kildare 7th Brigade stood as:

> Staff Officers: OC Tom Lawler; Adjutant Patrick Tuite; Quartermaster P. Kelly.
>
> 1st Battalion – Kill, Eadestown, Naas, Sallins and Clane Companies [Sallins and Clane were formed after the Truce was signed]. OC William Daly; Vice-OC Jim Dunne; Adj. M. Flanagan.
>
> 2nd Battalion – Newbridge area. OC O'Donoghue; Vice-OC Syl Ahearne.
>
> 3rd Battalion – Ballymore area. OC Martin O'Neill; Vice-OC T. Byrne; Adj. A. Metcalfe.
>
> 4th Battalion – Prosperous area. OC Edward Treacy; Vice-OC Thomas McHugh.
>
> 5th Battalion – Rathangan/Bracknagh area. OC M. Ryan; Vice-OC Jack Kenny.
>
> 6th Battalion – Brownstown/Kilcullen area. OC William Byrne; Vice-OC Paddy Brennan.[2]

The monthly police report for July 1921 commented, 'Since the Truce, the county has been very quiet,' while for August it noted, 'the terms of the Truce have been very well observed by the rebels in this county'. Through August and September recruits were drilled and given instruction in battle tactics, while intelligence gathering and arms procurement continued. On 20 August 1921 a party of about fifty IRA men forcibly took possession of Harristown House, an untenanted mansion belonging to the estate of the late Percy la Touche, and used it as a barracks. The IRA in Kildare continued to recruit and train for a return to war, with training camps set up in Celbridge and Athy.[3]

Shortly after the Truce, the IRA secured an office in Naas Town Hall and republican police went on duty in the town. They began their work quite professionally; for instance when two British Lancers accosted a young female on the road from Sallins to Clane, they were arrested by the republican police and handed over to the IRA, who in turn handed them over to their regiment. During the war the two soldiers could have been shot out of hand.[4] Some weeks later, the RIC received a tribute from the IRA, when Naas police barracks was being handed over to republicans. The senior RIC officer speaking to the IRA commander stated that the new government could have had almost the entire constabulary as its police force. The republican replied, 'But if we hadn't dealt with the RIC there would have been no Free State. We weren't afraid of the army. We could always fool them, but you fellows had the most marvellous local knowledge, which was too much for us. Anyhow, we want to have our police force modelled on your lot.'[5]

Following a raid on Kilmorony House, Athy, in early October 1921, a public remonstrance was made to Sinn Féin. Around thirty masked men raided the home of Lady Weldon, searching for arms. There were none and they left with field glasses and little else as Lady Weldon protested her patriotism. The Weldons were an Anglo-Irish family with a long military tradition. Many military families began to leave the county as officers returned to England and there were fears for the safety of those remaining. Because of the military garrisons and its rich land, Kildare had one of the highest percentages of Protestants in the south. With the changing times many loyalists no longer felt safe and they began making arrangements to move.[6]

On 26 August 1921 the Second Dáil met in public session to elect its president and ministry. All deputies present took the oath to serve and defend a thirty-two-county Irish Republic. Éamon de Valera was elected president, while the election of the cabinet proved the confidence of the Dáil in those who had been its leaders through what was known as the War of Independence. The following were re-elected as ministers: Arthur Griffith (Foreign Affairs), Austin Stack (Home Affairs), Cathal Brugha (Defence), Michael Collins (Finance), W. T. Cosgrave (Local Government) and Robert Barton (Economic Affairs). The following were appointed ministers outside the cabinet: Count George Plunkett (Fine Arts), Kevin O'Higgins (to assist Cosgrave in Local Government), Desmond Fitzgerald (Propaganda), J. J. O'Kelly (Education), Constance Markievicz (Labour), Ernest Blythe (Trade and Commerce), Art O'Connor (Agriculture) and Seán Etchingham (Fisheries).[7]

As peace negotiations between the Irish and British delegations began, the machinery of war continued to unwind. The workhouse buildings in Celbridge were occupied by the IRA, while the police barracks at Kilcullen and Monasterevin were evacuated.[8] The RIC held the first ever sports day and dance, which was attended by large components of police from around the county, in Naas Military Barracks in October. The following month hundreds of uniformed IRA men and Cumann na mBan women attended a commemoration in Barrowhouse, Athy, for the two local Volunteers killed in action the previous May.[9]

Arthur Griffith led the Irish delegation to Britain to negotiate the Treaty. De Valera stayed in Ireland, aware that there would have to be compromise and if a concession had to be made he did not want to be the one to make it. Second in command of the delegation was Michael Collins, who at first resisted the assignment and only gave in when he was convinced that it was his duty to go. The other members of the team were George Gavan Duffy, who had been a Sinn Féin representative in Paris; Eamonn Duggan, a solicitor who had acted as a front for Collins in Dublin; and Robert Barton, Minister of Economic Affairs, who as a landowner and an ex-English public schoolboy would understand the background and mentality of the men they would face in negotiation. Erskine Childers travelled to London as secretary of the Irish delegation. One of the most brilliant political manipulators of all time, David Lloyd George, headed the British team. Behind him were two men of great political stature: Winston Churchill and Lord Birkenhead (F. E. Smith).[10]

In London, Collins stayed in Cadogan Gardens, while Griffith and the other delegates resided in Hans Place. Collins had his own intelligence agents and bodyguards with him, among them Ned Broy, Emmett Dalton, Liam Tobin and Joe Dolan. David Neligan's cover remained intact and he was brought over to London by the British to spy on Collins![11]

Negotiations continued for several weeks and it became increasingly obvious to the Irish delegates that they would have to compromise with Britain. The delegates were in regular contact with de Valera and Sinn Féin, but as negotiators they were simply outclassed. Finally Lloyd George presented them with a Treaty and pressured them into accepting it under the threat of 'war within three days'.[12]

Collins remained in London for two further meetings on financial matters, but the Irish plenipotentiaries returned to Dublin on 3 December to discuss with de Valera Britain's final offer. They were told it was unacceptable. Yet, they, including Michael Collins, signed the Articles of Agreement on 6 December 1921. In explanation, Robert Barton wrote: 'The English Prime Minister ... declared that the signature and recommendation of every member of our delegation was necessary or war would follow immediately.'[13]

The two stumbling blocks were the loss of Ulster and the Oath of Allegiance. Both negotiating teams agreed that Ulster should give its decision, for or against union with the south, within one calendar month of the passing of the Irish Free State (Consequential Provisions) Act, 1922 – passed on 5 December 1922. The oath, finally agreed to and incorporated into the Treaty, read:

> I ... do solemnly swear true faith and allegiance to the Constitution of the Irish Free State as by law established, and that I will be faithful to H. M. King George V, his heirs and successors by law, in virtue of the common citizenship of Ireland with Great Britain and her adherence to and membership of the group of nations forming the British Commonwealth of Nations.[14]

There was to be no Irish Republic, only a Free State comprising twenty-six counties, with dominion status akin to that of Canada and Australia. The deal allowed for a greater deal of self-government than Home Rule, but fell short of the republic that had been proclaimed at Easter 1916.

The signing of the Treaty generated great rejoicing in the country. The IRA paraded openly in Athy, while in mid-December three battalions totalling 1,500 men of the 7th Kildare Brigade paraded on the Little Curragh. They demonstrated in signals, engineering and first aid and performed military drills, 'showing the efficiency and good appearance of the men as they marched past'.[15]

A special meeting of Kildare County Council was summoned on 30 December 1921 to consider the terms of the Treaty. Ten councillors were present. One, James O'Connor, did not attend. After much discussion a motion was proposed by Jack Fitzgerald, seconded by Henry Fay and supported by Councillors Michael Fitzsimons, Hugh Colohan and Nicholas Travers:

> That we, the Kildare County Council, are in favour of the ratification of the Treaty between Ireland and England, and call upon the Deputies for Kildare and Wicklow to support it.
>
> That copies of this resolution be sent to the Deputies for Kildare and Wicklow, and to Messrs. Griffith, de Valera and Collins.

The motion was declared and carried. Éamon Ó Modhrain dissented and Tom Harris did not vote.[16]

When the Irish delegates returned to Ireland, they found

public opinion on the Treaty sharply divided. The majority of ordinary people were relieved that the 'Troubles' had ended and that Ireland had achieved a measure of independence. However, others saw the Treaty as a sell-out and de Valera stated that the delegates should not have signed. Other Sinn Féin ministers felt that nothing less than a thirty-two-county republic, with no links to Britain, should have been accepted. The scene was set for a bitter split between those who supported the Treaty and those opposed to it. The Dáil approved the Treaty by sixty-four votes to fifty-seven. De Valera resigned as president and went into opposition to Griffith, who took his place. The Treaty stipulated that a Provisional Government chosen by the Parliament of Southern Ireland was to implement its terms and produce the Constitution of the Irish Free State.[17]

The mythical Irish Republic continued in being for a time, both in the minds of the supporters as well as opponents of the Treaty. The IRA, asserted the pro-Treaty Mulcahy, remained the army of the republic. Others who opposed the Treaty considered that they were defending the Irish Republic of 1916 and were the only ones entitled to the name 'Irish Republican Army'. In terms of County Kildare, the First Eastern Division, under its OC, Seán Boylan, was almost entirely pro-Treaty. There were pockets of republicans in Kildare, but of the nine brigades of the Division, only one – the 5th (Mullingar) Brigade – took the anti-Treaty side.[18]

The stage was set for Civil War and the resulting conflict saw more people killed in a shorter period of time than that of the War of Independence, not only throughout the country, but also in County Kildare.

CONCLUSION

The circumstances in Kildare from 1916–21 made it extremely difficult for the IRA to function, yet it did operate successfully and contributed enough generally to the overall campaign to get a commendation from IRA GHQ and sneaking admiration from the crown forces. Peter Hart in *The IRA at War 1916–1923* found that nine counties had similar or lower levels of IRA violence per 10,000 people than Kildare in the period 1917–23. The main areas of conflict in the War of Independence were Cork, Dublin, Tipperary, Limerick, Clare and Longford. Hart shows that revolutionary violence in County Kildare from 1917 to 1919 to be 0.0 violent republican incidents per 10,000 people; from 1920–1, 1.1 per 10,000 people; and 1921–1, 0.3 per 10,000 people.[1] He measures the violence in terms of its victims: those killed or wounded by bombs and bullets. However, raids on private homes, vandalism, assaults and robberies are not counted and for most of this period they were not reported.

Diarmuid Ferriter in *The Transformation of Ireland 1900–2000* writes: 'the revolution was as much regional as it was national in nature and much could depend on the traditions of radicalism within particular rural or urban areas, the relative wealth of a particular district or the strength of family connections'.[2] Families were very important (like the Hales of Cork), as were individuals such as Seán McEoin, Tom Barry, Dan Breen and Seán Treacy. Kildare had no one of this stature, but it did have prominent and dedicated activists such as Domhnall Ua Buachalla, Tom Harris and Jimmy Dunne. Dunne was only coming into his own in 1920 and became more prominent in 1922–3.

Terence Dooley, in his detailed contribution to the debate in 'IRA activity in Kildare during the War of Independence', writes:

> This chapter has pointed to the circumstances which made it extremely difficult for the IRA to operate in County Kildare. The IRA attracted very few members. For social, economic and even what could loosely be termed cultural reasons, its support base was a limited one. It was poorly armed and forced to fight in geographical terrain that was not conducive to guerrilla warfare. And it was faced with a military presence which severely restricted movement and organisation. Yet, the IRA did operate in the county and while it did not carry out the type of military operations of the IRA further south, it certainly made enough of a nuisance of itself to pin down crown forces that might have been deployed elsewhere. This was particularly true in the months leading up to the truce when the number of 'small jobs' escalated. Perhaps more significantly, the IRA and its supporters in Kildare seem to have been remarkably successful in the intelligence war and the information passed on to GHQ enabling the breaking of codes was undoubtedly of some importance.[3]

In County Kildare, the War of Independence resulted in the deaths of eleven people, large-scale raids (from both sides), hundreds of arrests, the destruction of much material and buildings, and upset to the lives of thousands of people. Measured against counties like Cork and Tipperary, or Dublin city, the violence may have been relatively moderate, and indeed less successful, but considering the obstacles faced by the republicans in the county it was nonetheless impressive. But the years 1919–21 in Kildare set the tone for the subsequent Civil War, when violence and the death toll in the county jumped four-fold.

NOTES

INTRODUCTION

1. Hopkinson, M., *The Irish War of Independence* (Dublin, 2002), p. 145.

1. REPUBLICANISM AND NATIONALISM IN KILDARE 1795–1913

1. Durney, James, 'The causes of the 1798 Rebellion in County Kildare', essay available in Kildare Library and Arts Service, Newbridge Library, Newbridge, County Kildare.
2. Corrigan, Mario, *All that Delirium of the Brave – Kildare in 1798* (Naas, 1997), p. 83.
3. *Ibid.*, p. 92.
4. Chambers, Liam, *Rebellion in Kildare, 1790–1803* (Dublin, 1998), pp. 102–6.
5. Ferriter, Diarmuid, The *Transformation of Ireland 1900–2000* (London 2004) p. 29.
6. Cullen, Seamus, *The Emmet Rising in Kildare. Conspiracy, Rebellion and Manhunt in County Kildare 1802–1806* (Dublin, 2004), pp. 37–41.
7. *Ibid.*, pp. 47–9.
8. *Ibid.*, pp. 55, 67, 86.
9. Chambers, *Rebellion in Kildare, 1790–1803*, p. 119.
10. Cullen, *The Emmet Rising in Kildare*, pp. 229–30; Corry, Eoghan, 'The Insurrection Act of 1807', *Kildare Voice*, 5 October 2007.

11. Corry, 'The Insurrection Act of 1807'.

12. Gibson, William H. & Nolan, Patrick F., 'Military influence on Kildare towns', *The Nationalist Centenary 1883–1983*, supplement (Newbridge, 1983).

13. Duffy, Seán, *Atlas of Irish History* (Dublin, 2000), p. 133.

14. Robinson, James, 'Terence McDonald (1810–1874), tithe farmer, Jigginstown, Naas, County Kildare. A study of person and place', essay, sourced at Kildare Library and Arts Service, Newbridge Library, Newbridge, County Kildare.

15. Duffy, *Atlas of Irish History*, p. 84.

16. Taaffe, Frank, 'Daniel O'Connell and Mullaghmast meeting', *The Nationalist*, 1 October 1993.

17. Kiely, Karel, *Tracing your Ancestors in Kildare* (Kildare, 1992), p. 13.

18. Comerford, R.V. *et al.*, *Lest We Forget. Kildare in the Great Famine* (Kildare, 1995), p. 57.

19. *Ibid.*, p. 70.

20. *Ibid.*, pp. 12–13.

21. Duffy, *Atlas of Irish History*, p. 106.

22. Moody, T. W. & Martin, F. X. (eds), *The Course of Irish History* (Dublin, 1994), p. 449.

23. Durney, James, Corrigan, Mario & Curran, Seamus (eds), *A Forgotten Hero. John Devoy* (Naas, 2008), p. 12.

24. Duffy, *Atlas of Irish History*, p. 96

25. Durney *et al.*, *A Forgotten Hero*, p. 16.

26. Duffy, *Atlas of Irish History*, p. 106.

27. Ryan, Mary, *The Clongorey Evictions* (Naas, 2001), p. 21.

28. *Ibid.*, pp. 56–7.

29. *Ibid.*, pp. 57–66.

30. *Ibid.*, pp. 72–3.

31. *Ibid.*, p. 78.

32. Coogan, Tim Pat, *1916. The Easter Rising* (Dublin, 2001), p. 18.

33. Durney, James, *On the One Road. Political Unrest in Kildare 1913–94* (Naas, 2001), p. 10.

34. Boyce, D. George, *Nationalism in Ireland* (London, 1982), p. 240.

35. *Ibid.*, p. 251.

36. Byrne, Michael, 'A paper with a mission', *Leinster Leader*, Centenary Supplement 1880–1980.

37. *Ibid.*

38. *The Kildare Observer*, 17 October 1891.

39. Moody & Martin, *The Course of Irish History*, p. 456.

40. *Leinster Leader*, 27 July 1895 & 3 August 1895; *The Kildare Observer*, 27 July 1895.

41. Clark, Samuel & Donnelly, James S. (eds), *Irish Peasants. Violence and Political Unrest 1780–1914* (Dublin, 1983), pp. 380–4.

42. Hopkinson, *The Irish War of Independence*, p. 12; *Leinster Leader*, 19 August 1922.

43. Coogan, *1916. The Easter Rising*, p. 29; *The Kildare Observer*, 5 April 1919.

44. Coogan, *1916. The Easter Rising*, pp. 16–17.

2. KILDARE RISING

1. McNally, Michael, *Easter Rising 1916. Birth of the Irish Republic* (Oxford, 2007), pp. 9–10.

2. Ferriter, *Transformation of Ireland 1900–2000*, pp. 166, 171.

3. McNally, *Easter Rising 1916*, p. 12.

4. Coogan, *1916. The Easter Rising*, p. 35.

5. Durney, *On the One Road*, p. 12.

6. Michael O'Kelly, witness statement 1155, Military Archives, Dublin.

7. McNally, *Easter Rising 1916*, pp. 11–12.

8. Ó Dubhghaill, M., *Insurrection Fires at Easter Tide* (Cork, 1966), p. 75.

9. Coogan, *1916. The Easter Rising*, p. 50.

10. Michael O'Kelly, witness statement 1155, Military Archives, Dublin; *Leinster Leader*, 12 September 1914.

11. Mac Giolla Choille, B., *1913–16. Intelligence Notes and List of Persons Sentenced by Court Martial 1916* (Dublin, 1966), p. 112.

12. Michael O'Kelly, witness statement 1155, Military Archives, Dublin.

13. *Ibid.*

14. Michael Smyth, witness statement 1531, Military Archives, Dublin.

15. Durney, *On the One Road*, p. 16.

16. Domhnall Ua Buachalla, witness statement 194, Military Archives, Dublin.

17. Michael Smyth, witness statement 1531, Military Archives, Dublin; Mac Giolla Choille, *1913–16. Intelligence Notes and List of Persons Sentenced by Court Martial 1916*, p. 179.

18. Durney, *On the One Road*, pp. 17–18.

19. *Ibid.*, pp. 18–19.

20. *Sunday Independent*, 23 April 1916.

21. Michael Smyth, witness statement 1531, Military Archives, Dublin.

22. Michael O'Kelly, witness statement 1155, Military Archives, Dublin.

23. James Dunne, witness statement 1571, Military Archives, Dublin.

24. Tom Harris, witness statement 320, Kildare Library and Arts Service, Newbridge Library, Newbridge, County Kildare.

25. Patrick Colgan, witness statement 850, Kildare Library and Arts Service, Newbridge Library, Newbridge, County Kildare.

26. Durney, *On the One Road*, p. 24.

27. *Ibid.*, p. 24.

28. McGarry, F., *Rebels. Voices from the Easter Rising* (London, 2011), p. 161.

29. Durney, *On the One Road*, pp. 24–8. Carrisvilla, County Kildare, is given as the birthplace of Private James Duffy, but there is no town, village or townland with that name on record.

30. Costello, Con, 'Wheeler of Robertstown', Looking Back Series no. 1084, *Leinster Leader*, 29 August 2002.

31. Durney, *On the One Road*, p. 28.

32. Coogan, *1916. The Easter Rising*, pp. 135–6.

33. *The Kildare Observer*, 2 May 1916.

34. Byrne, 'A paper with a mission'.

35. *Leinster Leader*, 6 May 1916.

36. Kildare County Council. Minutes of the County Council and its Committees. January–December 1916.

37. Flynn, B., *Pawns in the Game. Irish Hunger Strikes 1912–1981* (Cork, 2011), pp. 13–14.

38. Durney, *On the One Road*, pp. 32–3.

39. O'Mahony, S., *Frongoch. University of Revolution* (Dublin, 1987), p. 19.

3. WHO FEARS TO SPEAK OF EASTER WEEK?

1. O'Mahony, *Frongoch*, pp. 18–19.

2. Durney, *On the One Road*, p. 37.

3. *Ibid.*, p. 20.

4. *Ibid.*, pp. 37–8.

5. O'Mahony, *Frongoch*, pp. 122, 126.

6. *Ibid.*, pp. 19, 38, 117–25.

7. *Ibid.*, pp. 205–6.

8. *Ibid.*, pp. 38, 52, 58, 63; Patrick Colgan, witness statement 850, Kildare Library and Arts Service, Newbridge Library, Newbridge, County Kildare.

9. Durney, *On the One Road*, pp. 39–40.

10. *Leinster Leader*, 27 May 1916.

11. Coogan, T. P., *Ireland in the Twentieth Century* (London, 2003), p. 63.

12. O'Mahony, *Frongoch*, pp. 165–8.

13. Domhnall Ua Buachalla, witness statement 194, Military Archives, Dublin.

14. Michael Smyth, witness statement 1531, Military Archives, Dublin.

15. Smyth, Michael, 'Kildare battalions – 1920', *Capuchin Annual*, 1969.

16. Michael Smyth, witness statement 1531, Military Archives, Dublin.

17. Coogan, *Ireland in the Twentieth Century*, p. 66.

18. *Leinster Leader*, 18 August 1917.

19. Flynn, *Pawns in the Game*, pp. 24–6; *Leinster Leader*, 25 August 1997.

20. Corry, E., *Kildare GAA. A Centenary History* (Newbridge, 1984), p. 114.

21. Michael Smyth, witness statement 1531, Military Archives, Dublin.

22. Coogan, *Ireland in the Twentieth Century*, p. 67.

23. *Ibid.*, p. 67; Hopkinson, *The Irish War of Independence*, p. 14.

24. Michael Smyth, witness statement 1531, Military Archives, Dublin.

25. James Dunne, witness statement 1571, Military Archives, Dublin.

26. Patrick O'Carroll, witness statement 1161, Military Archives, Dublin.

27. Durney, *On the One Road*, pp. 42–3.

28. Michael O'Kelly, witness statement 1155, Military Archives, Dublin.

29. *Leinster Leader*, 13 April 1918.

30. Mitchell, A. & Ó Snodaigh, P., *Irish Political Documents, 1916–1949* (Dublin, 1985), pp. 41–2.

31. Copy of anti-conscription pledge, author's collection.

32. Costello, C., *A Most Delightful Station. The British Army on the Curragh of Kildare, Ireland, 1855–1922* (Cork, 1996), p. 311.

33. Durney, *On the One Road*, p. 43.

34. *Leinster Leader*, 20 April 1918.

35. Michael O'Kelly, witness statement 1155, Military Archives, Dublin.

36. Durney, *On the One Road*, p. 43.

37. *Leinster Leader*, 24 August 1918.

38. Michael O'Kelly, witness statement 1155, Military Archives, Dublin.

39. McGuire, J. & Quinn, J. (eds), *Dictionary of Irish Biography* (Cambridge, 2009), p. 229.

40. Michael O'Kelly, witness statement 1155, Military Archives, Dublin.

41. James Dunne, witness statement 1571, Military Archives, Dublin.

42. Corry, *Kildare GAA*, p. 114; Dwyer, T. R., *The Squad and the Intelligence Operations of Michael Collins* (Cork, 2005), pp. 10–12.

43. *Leinster Leader*, 12 October 1918.

44. *The Kildare Observer*, 16 November 1918; *Leinster Leader*, 16 November 1918.

45. Horne, J. (ed.), *Our War. Ireland and the Great War* (Dublin, 2008), p. 211.

46. Mitchell & Ó Snodaigh, *Irish Political Documents*, pp. 51–2; Michael O'Kelly, witness statement 1155, Military Archives, Dublin; *The Kildare Observer*, 7 December 1918.

47. Michael O'Kelly, witness statement 1155, Military Archives, Dublin; *The Kildare Observer*, 14 December 1918.

48. Michael O'Kelly, witness statement 1155, Military Archives, Dublin.

49. O'Keefe, Patrick, 'My reminiscences of 1914–23', *Oughterany. Journal of the Donadea Local History Group*, vol. 1, no. 1, 1993.

50. *The Kildare Observer*, 4 January 1919.

51. Mitchell & Ó Snodaigh, *Irish Political Documents*, pp. 53–4.

4. WAR COMES TO KILDARE

1. Dooley, Terence, 'IRA activity in Kildare during the War of Independence', in William Nolan & Thomas McGrath (eds), *Kildare. History and Society* (Dublin, 2006), p. 647.

2. *The Kildare Observer*, 4 January 1919 & 8 February 1919.

3. Durney, *On the One Road*, p. 46.

4. Breen, D., *My Fight for Irish Freedom* (Dublin, 1978), pp. 41–2; *The Kildare Observer*, 18 January 1919.

5. *Leinster Leader*, 15 February 1919.

6. Hopkinson, *The Irish War of Independence*, p. 26; *Leinster Leader*, 26 January 1962.

7. Hopkinson, *The Irish War of Independence* p. 40; *The Kildare Observer*, 5 April 1919.

8. *Dictionary of Irish Biography*, pp. 229–30.

9. Hanley, B., *The IRA. A Documentary History 1916–2005* (Dublin, 2010), p. 12; McCall, E., *The Auxiliaries. Tudor's Toughs* (Newtownards, 2010), p. 27.

10. *The Kildare Observer*, 5 July 1919.

11. *Ibid.*, 22 February 1919 & 16 March 1919.

12. *Ibid.*, 12 April 1919 & 3 May 1919.

13. Durney, *On the One Road*, p. 49.

14. Costello, *A Most Delightful Station*, p. 311.

15. *The Kildare Observer*, 26 July 1919.

16. *Ibid.*, 5 July 1919.

17. Colgan, John, 'Leixlip chronology 1900–2002', sourced on County Kildare Electronic History Journal; *The Kildare Observer*, 12 July 1919 & 26 July 1919.

18. Michael Smyth, witness statement 1531, Military Archives, Dublin.

19. Patrick Colgan, witness statement 850, Kildare Library and Arts Service, Newbridge Library, Newbridge, County Kildare.

20. *The Kildare Observer*, 23 August 1919.

21. *Ibid.*, 23 August 1919, 13 September 1919 & 29 October 1919.
22. Mitchell & Ó Snodaigh, *Irish Political Documents*, pp. 66–7; *The Kildare Observer*, 20 September 1919.
23. Coogan, T. P., *Michael Collins* (London, 1990), p. 119.
24. James Dunne, witness statement 1571, Military Archives, Dublin.
25. Durney, *On the One Road*, pp. 49–50; *The Kildare Observer*, 31 May 1919.
26. Hopkinson, *The Irish War of Independence*, p. 44; Kee, R., *The Green Flag. Volume III: Ourselves Alone* (London, 1989), p. 92.
27. Dooley, 'IRA activity in Kildare during the War of Independence'; Costello, *A Most Delightful Station*, pp. 312–13.
28. Comerford, Thomas, 'County Kildare and the Irish quest for independence 1916-21', essay, sourced at Kildare Library and Arts Service, Newbridge Library, Newbridge, County Kildare.
29. Costello, *A Most Delightful Station*, pp. 312–13.

5. A DEPLORABLE STATE

1. Bennett, R., *The Black and Tans* (New York, 1995), pp. 37–8, 71–2; Kee, *The Green Flag*, p. 96.
2. Michael O'Kelly, witness statement 1155, Military Archives, Dublin.
3. Costello, *A Most Delightful Station*, p. 315; *Leinster Leader*, 3 May 1969.
4. Bennett, *The Black and Tans*, p. 36.
5. *The Kildare Observer*, 5 & 19 June 1920; *Leinster Leader* 6 & 13 March 1920, 3 April 1920.
6. Kee, *The Green Flag*, p. 102; *The Kildare Observer* 10 & 17 April 1920; Michael Smyth, witness statement 1531, Military Archives, Dublin.
7. Hogan, David, *The Four Glorious Years* (Dublin, 1953), pp. 179–80.
8. Bennett, *The Black and Tans*, p. 40; Carey, T., *Mountjoy. The Story of a Prison* (Cork, 2005), pp. 185–6.

9. *The Kildare Observer*, 17 April 1920.

10. Carey, *Mountjoy*, pp. 186–7; *The Kildare Observer*, 9 May 1920.

11. *The Kildare Observer*, 17 April, 29 May & 19 June 1920.

12. Smyth, 'Kildare battalions – 1920'.

13. *The Kildare Observer*, 16 & 29 May 1920.

14. Patrick O'Carroll, witness statement 1161, Military Archives, Dublin.

15. *The Kildare Observer*, 5 June 1920.

16. Smyth, 'Kildare battalions – 1920'.

17. Durney, *On the One Road*, pp. 57–8, 64.

18. Kee, *The Green Flag*, p. 105; *The Kildare Observer*, 12 & 19 June 1920.

19. *Ibid.*, 12 June 1920.

20. Kildare County Council, Minute Book, No. 6, November 1919 to October 1920, sourced at Kildare Library and Arts Service, Newbridge Library, Newbridge County Kildare.

21. *The Irish Times*, 17 July 1920.

22. Bennett, *The Black and Tans*, p. 48.

23. *Ibid.*, p. 68; *The Irish Times* 18 & 20 July 1920.

24. McCall, *The Auxiliaries*, p. 31.

25. Smyth, 'Kildare battalions – 1920'; *The Irish Times*, 17 July 1920.

26. Leeson, D. M., *The Black and Tans. British Police and Auxiliaries in the Irish War of Independence* (Oxford, 2011), p. 10.

27. *The Irish Times*, 21 July 1920.

28. *Ibid.*, 22 July 1920.

29. *Ibid.*, 24 July 1920.

30. Leeson, *The Black and Tans*, p. 99

31. Kee, *The Green Flag*, p. 107; McCall, *The Auxiliaries*, pp. 43–4, 49, 51; Leeson, *The Black and Tans*, p. 99; Costello, *A Most Delightful Station*, p. 315.

32. Leeson, *The Black and Tans*, p. 29; *The Kildare Observer*, 28 August 1920.

33. Smyth, 'Kildare battalions – 1920'.

34. James Dunne, witness statement 1571, Military Archives, Dublin.

35. Dooley, 'IRA activity in Kildare during the War of Independence', p. 625.

36. James Dunne, witness statement 1571, Military Archives, Dublin.

37. *Leinster Leader*, 28 August 1920 & 4 September 1920; Abbott, Richard, *Police Casualties in Ireland 1919–1922* (Cork, 2000), p. 112.

38. *Leinster Leader*, 28 August 1920.

39. The late Ellen Mahon (1898–1979), great-aunt of the author, spoke to him of this incident many times; the author interviewed Frank Lawler, son of the late Peter Lawler, in August 2007.

40. *Leinster Leader*, 28 August 1920 & 11 September 1920.

41. *Ibid.*, 11 September 1920.

42. *Ibid.*, 4 September 1920.

43. *The Kildare Observer*, 11 & 25 September 1920.

44. *Ibid.*, 2 & 9 October 1920.

45. *Leinster Leader*, 4 & 11 September, 11 October 1920.

46. *Ibid.*, 21 & 30 October 1920.

47. James Dunne, witness statement 1571, Military Archives, Dublin.

48. Smyth, 'Kildare battalions – 1920'; Maureen Cusack, as told to Executive Librarian Mario Corrigan, Newbridge Library, Newbridge, County Kildare, 13 July 2012.

49. *The Kildare Observer*, 20 November 1920; Smyth, 'Kildare battalions – 1920'.

50. Smyth, 'Kildare Battalions – 1920'; *Leinster Leader*, 20 November & 12 December 1920.

51. Kee, *The Green Flag*, p. 119; Durney, *On the One Road*, pp. 68–9.

52. Doohan, T., *A History of Celbridge* (Celbridge, 2011), p. 106; GAA Museum, Croke Park.

53. *Leinster Leader*, 27 November 1920; Dwyer, *The Squad and the Intelligence Operations of Michael Collins*, pp. 186–8.

54. *The Irish Times*, 24 November 1920.

55. Durney, *On the One Road*, p. 70.

56. O'Halpin, Eunan, 'Counting terror: Bloody Sunday and the dead of the Irish revolution,' in D. Fitzpatrick (ed.), *Terror in Ireland 1916–1923* (Dublin, 2012), p. 145.

57. Smyth, 'Kildare battalions – 1920'.

58. Taaffe, F., *Eye on Athy's Past* (Athy, 2000), pp. 68–9.

59. Smyth, 'Kildare Battalions – 1920'.

60. *Ibid.*; *The Kildare Observer*, 25 December 1920.

61. Townshend, C., *The British Campaign in Ireland 1919–21. The Development of Political and Military Policies* (Oxford, 1975), p. 140; Mitchell, A., *Revolutionary Government in Ireland. Dáil Éireann, 1919–22* (Dublin, 1995), p. 171.

6. SHEEP, SINN FÉINERS AND SOLDIERS

1. Dooley, 'IRA activity in Kildare during the War of Independence', p. 636; Gibson & Nolan, 'Military influence on Kildare towns'.

2. Durney, James, *A Bridge, a Town, a People. Social Housing in Newbridge 1900–1996* (Naas, 2009), pp. 14, 17.

3. Costello, *A Most Delightful Station*, pp. 23–4.

4. Gibson & Nolan, 'Military influence on Kildare towns'; Durney, J., 'The Dubs come to Naas,' County Kildare Online Electronic History Journal, 21 July 2012.

5. Muenger, E. A., *The British Military Dilemma in Ireland. Occupation Politics, 1886–1914* (Dublin, 1991), pp. 4–5.

6. Durney, James, *Far from the Short Grass. The Story of Kildaremen in the Two World Wars* (Naas, 2001) p. 119.

7. Donohoe, Ann & Herrievan Eric, 'Price family of Newbridge, 1895–1989', April 1989, sourced at Kildare Library and Arts Service, Newbridge Library, Newbridge, County Kildare.

8. Census of Ireland, 1911, sourced at Kildare Library and Arts Service, Newbridge Library, Newbridge, County Kildare.

9.   Dooley, 'IRA activity in Kildare during the War of Independence', p. 642; Costello, *A Most Delightful Station*, pp. 178–9.

10. Michael O'Kelly, witness statement 1155, Military Archives, Dublin.

11. *The Kildare Observer*, 15 February 1919.

12. *Ibid.*, 8 March 1919.

13. Kenny, Liam, 'The politics of Punchestown', Looking Back Series no. 225, *Leinster Leader*, 19 April 2011.

14. *The Kildare Observer*, 15 March 1919.

15. *Ibid.*, 22 March 1919; Costello, *A Most Delightful Station*, p. 311.

16. Dooley, 'IRA activity in Kildare during the War of Independence', p. 633.

17. Bence Jones, M., *Twilight of the Ascendancy* (London, 1993), pp. 190, 202.

18. *The Kildare Observer*, 14 August 1920.

19. Bence Jones, *Twilight of the Ascendancy*, p. 190.

20. Costello, 'Wheeler of Robertstown'.

21. Bence Jones, *Twilight of the Ascendancy*, pp. 204–5; *The New York Times*, 2 April 1921.

7. NO ORDINARY WOMEN: CUMANN NA MBAN IN KILDARE

1.   McCarthy, C., *Cumann na mBan and the Irish Revolution 1914–1923* (Dublin, 2007), p. 5.

2.   *Ibid.*, p. 16.

3.   *Ibid.*, pp. 14–5.

4.   *Ibid.*, p. 12.

5.   *Ibid.*, p. 16.

6.   *Ibid.*, p. 17.

7.   *Ibid.*, p. 26.

8.   *Leinster Leader*, 29 August 1914.

9. Matthews, Ann, *Renegades: Irish Republican Women 1900–1922* (Cork 2010), pp. 101–2.

10. Matthews, Ann, 'Redressing the balance. Cumann na mBan 1913–26', unpublished MA Thesis (1995), sourced at NUI Maynooth.

11. Brigid O'Mullane, witness statement 450, Military Archives, Dublin.

12. *Ibid.*; Bulmer Hobson, witness statement 52, Military Archives, Dublin.

13. Cullen Owens, R., *A Social History of Women in Ireland. 1870–1970* (Dublin, 2005) p. 116.

14. Matthews, *Renegades: Irish Republican Women 1900–1922*, p. 108; McCarthy, *Cumann na mBan and the Irish Revolution 1914–1923*, p. 35.

15. McCarthy, *Cumann na mBan and the Irish Revolution 1914–1923*, pp. 45–6.

16. *Ibid.*, p. 49.

17. *Ibid.*, pp. 49, 54–5, 59.

18. Durney, *On the One Road*, p. 42.

19. Cullen Owens, *A Social History of Women in Ireland*, p. 116.

20. Matthews, *Renegades: Irish Republican Women 1900–1922*, pp. 236–9.

21. Luddy, M., *Women in Ireland, 1800–1918* (Cork, 2005), p. 244.

22. Durney, *On the One Road*, pp. 56–7.

23. Matthews, 'Redressing the balance. Cumann na mBan 1913–26'.

24. Durney, *On the One Road*, p. 78.

25. James Dunne, witness statement 1571, Military Archives, Dublin.

26. McCarthy, *Cumann na mBan and the Irish Revolution 1914–1923*, p. 164.

27. McCoole, S., *No Ordinary Women. Irish Female Activists in the Revolutionary Years 1900–1923* (Dublin, 2004), p. 83.

28. *Ibid.*, pp. 218–38.

29. Matthews, 'Redressing the balance. Cumann na mBan 1913–26'.

8. THE INTELLIGENCE WAR

1. Eamon Broy, witness statement 1280, Military Archives, Dublin.

2. McGuire & Quinn, *Dictionary of Irish Biography*, pp. 942–3; 'Former Garda chief dies at 85', *Irish Press*, 24 January 1972.

3. Eamon Broy, witness statement 1280, Military Archives, Dublin.

4. McGuire & Quinn, *Dictionary of Irish Biography*, pp. 942–3.

5. Eamon Broy, witness statement 1280, Military Archives, Dublin.

6. Coogan, *Michael Collins*, p. 107.

7. *Ibid.*, pp. 117–18; Dwyer, *The Squad and the Intelligence Operations of Michael Collins*, pp. 85–6.

8. Coogan, *Michael Collins*, p. 96.

9. Neligan, D., *The Spy in the Castle* (London, 1968), p. 78.

10. Durney, *On the One Road*, p. 59; McGuire & Quinn, *Dictionary of Irish Biography*, pp. 942–3.

11. Eamon Broy, witness statement 1280, Military Archives, Dublin.

12. Patrick Colgan, witness statement 850, Kildare Library and Arts Service, Newbridge Library, Newbridge, County Kildare.

13. Durney, *On the One Road*, p. 58.

14. Patrick Colgan, witness statement 850, Kildare Library and Arts Service, Newbridge Library, Newbridge, County Kildare; Kavanagh, Seán, 'The Irish Volunteers', *Capuchin Annual*, 1969.

15. Kavanagh, 'The Irish Volunteers'.

9. A CALICO SHACK IN KILDARE

1. Campbell, C., *Emergency Law in Ireland 1918–1925* (Oxford, 2005), p. i.

2. *Ibid.*, p. 15.

3. *Ibid.*, p. 105.

4. *The Kildare Observer*, 6 May 1916.

5. Crawford, Hugh, 'The internment camps', *The Curragh Revisited* (Curragh, 2002) p. 10.

6. *Ibid.*, pp. 10–11.
7. *Leinster Leader*, 12 March 1921.
8. Andrews, C. S., *Dublin Made Me* (Dublin, 1979), p. 173; Byrne, T., 'Famous jail escapes in Ireland', undated newspaper account in author's possession.
9. Andrews, *Dublin Made Me*, p. 173.
10. Hart, P. (ed.), *British Intelligence in Ireland, 1920–21. The Final Reports* (Cork, 2002), p. 26.
11. Campbell, *Emergency Law in Ireland 1918–1925*, p. 109.
12. *Leinster Leader*, 12 March 1921.
13. Byrne, 'Famous jail escapes in Ireland'.
14. Swan, Desmond (ed.), *Handbook of the Curragh Command* (Curragh, 1984), p. 21.
15. *An Cosantoir*, Curragh Commemorative Issue, May 1972, p. 64.
16. Andrews, *Dublin Made Me*, p. 174.
17. Behan, Thomas, *Poems* (Drogheda, 1923). Copy given to author by Marie Maher, niece of Tom Behan.
18. Campbell, *Emergency Law in Ireland 1918–1925*, p. 110.
19. *Ibid.*, p. 110.
20. Andrews, *Dublin Made Me*, pp. 175–6.
21. Sheehan, W., *British Voices from the Irish War of Independence 1918–1921* (Cork, 2007), pp. 48–51.
22. *Leinster Leader*, 21 & 28 May 1921.
23. Sheehan, *British Voices from the Irish War of Independence 1918–1921*, pp. 48–51.
24. *An Cosantoir*, Curragh Commemorative Issue, p. 64.
25. Copy of original document, donated by Karen Woodstock, (uncategorised) in Kildare Library and Arts Service, Newbridge Library, Newbridge, County Kildare.
26. Sheehan, *British Voices from the Irish War of Independence 1918–1921*, p. 51.

27. *Leinster Leader*, 16 July 1921.

28. *An Cosantoir*, Curragh Commemorative Issue, p. 64.

29. Byrne, 'Famous jail escapes in Ireland'.

30. Durney, *On the One Road*, pp. 91–2.

31. As told to author, *c.* June 2001, by the late Enda Bracken, son of Peadar Bracken.

32. Durney, *On the One Road*, p. 92; *Leinster Leader*, 17 September 1921.

33. Durney, James, 'The Curragh internees, 1921–24: from defiance to defeat', *County Kildare Archaeological Society Journal*, vol. xx (part iii), 2010–2011, p. 14.

34. *Leinster Leader*, 29 October 1921.

35. Sheehan, *British Voices from the Irish War of Independence*, pp. 50–1.

36. *Leinster Leader*, 29 October 1921.

37. *Ibid.*

38. *Ibid.*, 29 November 1921 & 10 December 1921.

39. *Ibid.*, 10 December 1921.

10. WAR AND PEACE

1. Townshend, *The British Campaign in Ireland 1919–21*, pp. 44, 52, 211.

2. Hart, P., *The I.R.A. at War 1916–1923* (Oxford, 2003), pp. 112–13.

3. Bennett, *The Black and Tans*, p. 157.

4. *Ibid.*, p. 161.

5. *Leinster Leader*, 1 January 1921; O'Donovan, D., *Kevin Barry and his time* (Dublin, 1989), p. 52.

6. Smyth, 'Kildare battalions – 1920'.

7. Dooley, 'IRA activity in Kildare during the War of Independence', p. 635.

8. O'Keefe, 'My reminiscences of 1914–23'.

9. *The Kildare Observer*, 8 January 1921.

10. *Leinster Leader*, 15 January 1921.

11. Kildare County Council, Minute Book No. 9, 10 January 1921.

12. *Ibid.*, 12 January 1921.

13. The late Ellen Mahon (1898–1979), great-aunt of the author, spoke to him of this undated incident several times.

14. Hickey, Joe, 'How Hickey's of Calverstown got its name', in Narraghmore Local History Group, *The Griese Valley and Beyond* (Calverstown, 2003).

15. *Leinster Leader*, 15 January 1921.

16. *Ibid.*, 12 February 1921.

17. *Ibid.*, 5 & 12 February 1921.

18. *Ibid.*, 26 February 1921 & 5 March 1921; *The Kildare Observer*, 5 March 1921.

19. Smyth, 'Kildare battalions – 1920'.

20. Pat Sheehan, interview with the author, 2 March 2001.

21. *Leinster Leader*, 19 March 1921.

22. *Ibid.*, 5 & 19 March 1921.

23. Michael Smyth, witness statement 1531, Military Archives, Dublin; Durney, *On the One Road*, p. 76.

24. Dooley, 'IRA activity in Kildare during the War of Independence', pp. 635–6.

25. Hopkinson, *The Irish War of Independence*, p. 145.

26. Dooley, 'IRA activity in Kildare during the War of Independence', pp. 635–6.

27. Bicentenary Committee, St Peter's Church, *1790 St. Peter's Church, Two-Mile-House 1990* (Naas, 1990).

28. Dooley, 'IRA activity in Kildare during the War of Independence', pp. 635–6.

29. Kautt, W. H., *Ambushes and Armour. The Irish Rebellion 1919–1921* (Dublin, 2010), p. 160.

30. Patrick O'Carroll, witness statement 1161, Military Archives, Dublin.

31. *Ibid.*

32. James Dunne, witness statement 1571, Military Archives, Dublin; *Leinster Leader*, 2 April 1966.

33. *Leinster Leader*, 21 May 1921, 26 November 1921 & 23 November 1985.

34. Coogan, O., *Politics and War in Meath 1913–23* (Meath, 1983), pp. 173–6.

35. Abbott, *Police Casualties in Ireland 1919–1922*, pp. 242–3.

36. Kee, *The Green Flag*, p. 139.

37. *The Kildare Observer*, 21 May 1921.

38. *Leinster Leader*, 11 June 1921.

39. Costello, *A Most Delightful Station*, p. 320; *Leinster Leader*, 4 & 11 June 1921, 2 July 1921.

40. Smyth, 'Kildare battalions – 1920'; *The Irish Times*, 29 June 1921; *The Kildare Observer*, 18 June 1921. A relative of Michael Power (from Scotland) visited the area in question in 2001 and spoke to the author about the incident.

41. Corry, *Kildare GAA*, p. 117.

42. *The Irish Times*, 20 June 1921; *The Kildare Observer*, 25 June 1921. Conversation with the late Paddy Sheehan, *c.* April 2001, and Paddy Behan, *c.* March 2001.

43. *The Kildare Observer*, 25 June 1921.

44. *Ibid.*

45. *Ibid.*, 9 July 1921.

46. *Ibid.*

47. Michael Smyth, witness statement 1531, Military Archives, Dublin; *Leinster Leader*, 12 July 1958.

48. *Leinster Leader*, 9 July 1921; *The Kildare Observer*, 29 October 1921.

49. Bennett, *The Black and Tans*, pp. 212–18.

50. Mitchell & Ó Snodaigh, *Irish Political Documents*, p. 114.

51. First Eastern Division general order, copy in author's possession.

52.   *Leinster Leader*, 16 July 1921.

11. TRUCE AND TREATY

1.   Bennett, *The Black and Tans*, p. 221; Hanley, *The IRA*, p. 36.
2.   James Dunne, witness statement 1571, Military Archives, Dublin.
3.   Comerford, 'County Kildare and the Irish quest for independence 1916–21'.
4.   Durney, *On the One Road*, p. 88.
5.   McCall, *The Auxiliaries*, pp. 161–2.
6.   *The Kildare Observer*, 15 September 1921.
7.   Durney, *On the One Road*, pp. 88–9.
8.   *The Kildare Observer*, 15 & 29 October 1921.
9.   *Ibid.*, 8 October 1921; *Leinster Leader*, 29 November 1921.
10.   Kee, *The Green Flag*, pp. 149–50.
11.   Durney, *On the One Road*, p. 93.
12.   Pakenham, Frank, *Peace by Ordeal* (London, 1935), p. 298.
13.   Whyte's, *History, Literature and Collectibles*, catalogue, November 2012, p. 52.
14.   Kee, *The Green Flag*, pp. 150–5.
15.   *Leinster Leader*, 19 December 1921.
16.   Kildare County Council, Minute Book No. 9, 30 December 1921.
17.   Kee, *The Green Flag*, p. 157.
18.   MacEvilly, M. *A Splendid Resistance. The Life of IRA Chief of Staff Dr. Andy Cooney* (Dublin, 2011), p. 71.

CONCLUSION

1.   Hart, *The IRA at War 1916–1923*, pp. 35–6.
2.   Ferriter, *The Transformation of Ireland 1900–2000,* pp. 229–30.
3.   Dooley, 'IRA activity in Kildare during the War of Independence'.

BIBLIOGRAPHY

PRIMARY SOURCES

An Cosantoir. The Irish Defence Journal, Curragh Commemorative Issue, May 1972

Bloxham, Elizabeth, witness statement 632, Military Archives, Cathal Brugha Barracks, Dublin

Broy, Eamon, witness statement 1280, Military Archives, Cathal Brugha Barracks, Dublin

Census of Ireland, 1911, sourced at Kildare Library and Arts Service, Newbridge Library, Newbridge, County Kildare

Colgan, Patrick, witness statement 850, Kildare Library and Arts Service, Newbridge Library, Newbridge, County Kildare

Dunne, James, witness statement 1571, Military Archives, Cathal Brugha Barracks, Dublin

Harris, Tom, witness statement 320, Kildare Library and Arts Service, Newbridge Library, Newbridge, County Kildare

Hobson, Bulmer, witness statement 52, Military Archives, Cathal Brugha Barracks, Dublin

Kildare County Council, Minutes of the County Council and its Committees, January–December 1916, sourced at Kildare Library and Arts Service, Newbridge Library, Newbridge, County Kildare

— Minute Book, No. 9, November 1920–May 1924, sourced at Kildare Library and Arts Service, Newbridge Library, Newbridge, County Kildare

O'Carroll, Patrick, witness statement 1161, Military Archives, Cathal
    Brugha Barracks, Dublin
O'Kelly, Michael, witness statement 1155, Military Archives, Cathal
    Brugha Barracks, Dublin
O'Mullane, Brigid, witness statement 450, Military Archives, Cathal
    Brugha Barracks, Dublin
Smyth, Michael, witness statement 1531, Military Archives, Cathal
    Brugha Barracks, Dublin
Ua Buachalla, Domhnall, witness statement 194, Military Archives,
    Cathal Brugha Barracks, Dublin

NEWSPAPERS

Irish Press, The
Irish Times, The
Kildare Observer, The
Kildare Voice
Leinster Leader
Nationalist and Leinster Times, The
New York Times, The

BOOKS

Abbott, Richard, *Police Casualties in Ireland 1919–1922* (Cork, 2000)
Andrews, C. S., *Dublin Made Me* (Dublin, 1979)
Behan, Thomas, *Poems* (Drogheda, 1923)
Bence Jones, Mark, *Twilight of the Ascendancy* (London, 1993)
Bennett, Richard, *The Black and Tans* (New York, 1995)
Bicentenary Committee, St Peter's Church, *1790 St. Peter's Church,
    Two-Mile-House 1990* (Naas, 1990)
Boyce, D. George, *Nationalism in Ireland* (London, 1982)
Breen, Dan, *My Fight for Irish Freedom* (Dublin, 1978)

Campbell, Colm, *Emergency Law in Ireland 1918–1925* (Oxford, 2005)

Carey, Tim, *Mountjoy. The Story of a Prison* (Cork, 2005)

Chambers, Liam, *Rebellion in Kildare, 1790–1803* (Dublin, 1998)

Clark, Samuel & Donnelly, James S. (eds), *Irish Peasants. Violence and Political Unrest 1780–1914* (Dublin, 1983)

Comerford, R. V. *et al.*, *Lest We Forget. Kildare in the Great Famine* (Kildare, 1995)

Coogan, Oliver, *Politics and War in Meath 1913–23* (Meath, 1983)

Coogan, Tim Pat, *Michael Collins* (London, 1990)

— *1916. The Easter Rising* (Dublin, 2001)

— *Ireland in the Twentieth Century* (London, 2003)

Corrigan, Mario, *All that Delirium of the Brave – Kildare in 1798* (Naas, 1997)

Corry, Eoghan, *Kildare GAA. A Centenary History* (Newbridge, 1984)

Costello, Con, *A Most Delightful Station. The British Army on the Curragh of Kildare, Ireland, 1855–1922* (Cork, 1996)

Cullen, Seamus, *The Emmet Rising in Kildare. Conspiracy, Rebellion and Manhunt in County Kildare 1802–1806* (Dublin, 2004)

Cullen Owens, Rosemary, *A Social History of Women in Ireland 1870–1970* (Dublin, 2005)

Curragh Local History Group, *The Curragh Revisited* (Curragh, 2002)

Doohan, Tony, *A History of Celbridge* (Celbridge, 2011)

Duffy, Seán, *Atlas of Irish History* (Dublin, 2000)

Durney, James, *Far from the Short Grass. The Story of Kildaremen in the Two World Wars* (Naas, 2001)

— *On the One Road. Political unrest in Kildare 1913–94* (Naas, 2001)

— *A Bridge, a Town, a People. Social Housing in Newbridge 1900–1996* (Naas, 2009)

Durney, James, Corrigan, Mario & Curran, Seamus (eds), *A Forgotten Hero. John Devoy* (Naas, 2008)

Dwyer, T. Ryle, *The Squad and the Intelligence Operations of Michael Collins* (Cork, 2005)

Ferriter, Diarmuid, *The Transformation of Ireland 1900–2000* (London, 2004)

Fitzpatrick, D. (ed.), *Terror in Ireland 1916–1923* (Dublin, 2012)

Flynn, Barry, *Pawns in the Game. Irish Hunger Strikes 1912–1981* (Cork, 2011)

Hanley, Brian, *The IRA. A Documentary History 1916–2005* (Dublin, 2010)

Hart, Peter, *The I.R.A. at War 1916–1923* (Oxford, 2003)

— (ed.), *British Intelligence in Ireland, 1920–21. The Final Reports* (Cork, 2002)

Hogan, David, *The Four Glorious Years* (Dublin, 1953)

Hopkinson, Michael, *The Irish War of Independence* (Dublin, 2002)

Horne, John (ed.), *Our War. Ireland and the Great War* (Dublin, 2008)

Kautt, W. H., *Ambushes and Armour. The Irish Rebellion 1919–1921* (Dublin, 2010)

Kee, Robert, *The Green Flag. Volume III: Ourselves Alone* (London, 1989)

Kiely, Karel, *Tracing Your Ancestors in Kildare* (Kildare, 1992)

Knirck, Jason, *Women of the Dáil – Gender, Republicanism and the Anglo-Irish Treaty* (Dublin, 2006)

Leeson, D. M., *The Black and Tans. British Police and Auxiliaries in the Irish War of Independence* (Oxford, 2011)

Luddy, Maria, *Women in Ireland, 1800–1918* (Cork, 2005)

MacEvilly, Michael, *A Splendid Resistance. The Life of IRA Chief of Staff Dr. Andy Cooney* (Dublin, 2011)

Mac Giolla Choille, Brendán, *1913–16. Intelligence Notes and List of Persons Sentenced by Court Martial 1916* (Dublin, 1966)

Matthews, Ann, 'Redressing the balance. Cumann na mBan 1913–26', MA Thesis, copy in NUI Maynooth, L.O. 1427 (1995)

— *Renegades: Irish Republican Women 1900–1922* (Cork, 2010)

McCall, Ernest, *The Auxiliaries. Tudor's Toughs* (Newtownards, 2010)

McCarthy, Cal, *Cumann na mBan and the Irish Revolution 1914–1923* (Dublin, 2007)

McCoole, Sinéad, *No Ordinary Women. Irish Female Activists in the Revolutionary Years 1900–1923* (Dublin, 2004)

McGarry, Fearghal, *Rebels. Voices from the Easter Rising* (London, 2011)

McGuire, James & Quinn, James (eds), *Dictionary of Irish Biography* (Cambridge, 2009)

McNally, Michael, *Easter Rising 1916. Birth of the Irish Republic* (Oxford, 2007)

Mitchell, Arthur, *Revolutionary Government in Ireland. Dáil Éireann, 1919–22* (Dublin, 1995)

Mitchell, Arthur & Ó Snodaigh, Pádraig, *Irish Political Documents, 1916–1949* (Dublin, 1985)

Moody, T. W. & Martin, F. X. (eds), *The Course of Irish History* (Dublin, 1994)

Muenger, Elizabeth A., *The British Military Dilemma in Ireland. Occupation Politics, 1886–1914* (Dublin, 1991)

Narraghmore Local History Group, *The Griese Valley and Beyond* (Calverstown, 2003)

Neligan, David, *The Spy in the Castle* (London, 1968)

Nolan, William & McGrath, Thomas (eds), *Kildare. History and Society* (Dublin, 2006)

O'Donovan, Donal, *Kevin Barry and his Time* (Dublin, 1989)

Ó Dubhghaill, M., *Insurrection Fires at Easter Tide* (Cork, 1966)

O'Mahony, Seán, *Frongoch. University of Revolution* (Dublin, 1987)

Pakenham, Frank, *Peace by Ordeal* (London, 1935)

Ryan, Annie, *Comrades. Inside the War of Independence* (Dublin, 2007)

Ryan, Mary, *The Clongorey Evictions* (Naas, 2001)

Sheehan, William, *British Voices from the Irish War of Independence 1918–1921. The Words of British Servicemen Who Were There* (Cork, 2007)

Swan, Desmond (ed.), *Handbook of the Curragh Command* (Curragh, 1984)

Taaffe, Frank, *Eye on Athy's Past* (Athy, 2000)

Townshend, Charles, *The British Campaign in Ireland 1919–21. The Development of Political and Military Policies* (Oxford, 1975)

PAPERS/ARTICLES

Byrne, Capt. Thomas, 'Famous jail escapes in Ireland', undated newspaper account in author's possession

Byrne, Michael, 'A paper with a mission', *Leinster Leader*, Centenary Supplement 1880–1980

Colgan, John, 'Leixlip chronology 1900–2002', County Kildare Online Electronic History Journal, 24 November 2007

Comerford, Thomas, 'County Kildare and the Irish quest for independence 1916–21', essay, copy held in Kildare Library and Arts Service, Newbridge Library, Newbridge, County Kildare

Corry, Eoghan, 'The Insurrection Act of 1807', *Kildare Voice*, 5 October 2007

Costello, Con, 'Wheeler of Robertstown', Looking Back Series no. 1084, *Leinster Leader*, 29 August 2002

Crawford, Hugh, 'The internment camps', in *The Curragh Revisited*, Curragh Local History Group, 2002

Donohoe, Ann & Herrievan, Eric, 'Price family of Newbridge, 1895–1989', Heritage Research, Newbridge, April 1989, sourced at Kildare Library and Arts Service, Newbridge Library, Newbridge, County Kildare

Dooley, Terence, 'IRA activity in Kildare during the War of Independence', in William Nolan & Thomas McGrath (eds), *Kildare. History and Society* (Dublin, 2006)

Durney, James, 'The Curragh internees, 1921–24: from defiance to defeat', County Kildare Archaeological Society Journal, vol. xx (part iii), 2010–2011

— 'The causes of the 1798 Rebellion in County Kildare', essay, copy held in Kildare Library and Arts Service, Newbridge Library, Newbridge, County Kildare

— 'The effects of the Great Famine in Kildare 1845–50', essay, copy held in Kildare Library and Arts Service, Newbridge Library, Newbridge, County Kildare

— 'The Dubs come to Naas', County Kildare Online Electronic History Journal, 21 July 2012

Gibson, William H. & Nolan, Patrick. F., 'Military influence on Kildare towns,' *The Nationalist Centenary 1883–1983*, supplement (Newbridge, 1983)

Hickey, Joe, 'How Hickey's of Calverstown got its name', in Narraghmore Local History Group, *The Griese Valley and Beyond* (Calverstown, 2003)

Kavanagh, Seán, 'The Irish Volunteers', *Capuchin Annual*, 1969

Kenny, Liam, 'The politics of Punchestown', Looking Back Series no. 225, *Leinster Leader*, 19 April 2011

O'Halpin, Eunan, 'Counting terror: Bloody Sunday and the dead of the Irish revolution', in D. Fitzpatrick (ed.), *Terror in Ireland 1916– 1923* (Dublin, 2012)

O'Keefe, Patrick, 'My reminiscences of 1914–23', *Ougtheraney, Journal of the Donadea Local History Group*, vol. 1, no. 1, 1993

Robinson, James, 'Terence McDonald (1810–1874), tithe farmer, Jigginstown, Naas, County Kildare. A study of person and place', essay, sourced at Kildare Library and Arts Service, Newbridge Library, Newbridge, County Kildare

Smyth, Michael, 'Kildare battalions – 1920', *Capuchin Annual*, 1969

Taaffe, Frank, 'Daniel O'Connell and Mullaghmast meeting', *The Nationalist*, 1 October 1993

Whyte's, *History, literature and collectibles*, catalogue, November 2012

INTERVIEWS

Paddy Behan, local historian, various dates in 2001 and 2011

The late Enda Bracken, various dates in 2001

Maureen Cusack spoke to Mario Corrigan, 13 July 2012

The late Ellen Gaul (1898–1979) spoke to the author on numerous occasions of events in 1919–21

Frank Lawler, 30 August 2007

The late Marie Maher, Rathangan, 7 March 2001

The late Paddy Sheehan, Henry Street, Newbridge, various dates in 2001

INDEX